THE HUTCHINSON BOOK OF
KINGS AND
QUEENS
OF ENGLAND

Written by Tony Robinson

Illustrated by Tony Ross

With contributions from John Farman, Inga Moore, Doffy Weir,
Jonny Boatfield, Susie Jenkin-Pearce, Peter Weevers, Anthony Browne,
Babette Cole, Martina Selway, Shirley Hughes and Nicholas Allan

HUTCHINSON

London Sydney Auckland Johannesburg

Contents

942

Who invented the king of England?

England hasn't always had kings and queens, and the people who live in it haven't always called themselves the English. Two thousand years ago the whole country was divided into tribes, and you were loyal to your tribe and your tribe-chief. The word English didn't even exist.

Then the Romans invaded, and the country we call England became part of the Roman Empire. There was an emperor living somewhere across the sea in Rome, but still no king of England.

Eventually the Romans cleared off again. Why? Well, partly because they were fed up with being attacked by pirates from northern Europe who were landing all over the English coast. With the Romans gone, the pirates began to settle. They staked out their own territories under the leadership of their warlords. They were always squabbling and fighting each other, and gradually the stronger territories got bigger and bigger, until eventually there were only seven of them left covering the whole country. Around this time their leaders, who like leaders the world over wanted to show off, started calling themselves kings. But they still weren't kings of England. They were kings of the Northumbrians, or the Mercians or the East Saxons. Sometimes a king would become more powerful than the other kings, and to show how grand he was, he'd call himself the king of the English, although most people didn't take much notice.

But then something happened that changed everything. Boatloads of pirates from Norway, Denmark and Sweden began landing in England and they were fiercer and scarier than anything that anyone had seen before. They were called the Vikings, and pretty soon they had conquered half of England. If the squabbling tribesmen didn't sort themselves out, they'd find themselves with a very close haircut from a Viking war-axe – and there'd be no England at all.

It was then that the king of England was invented!

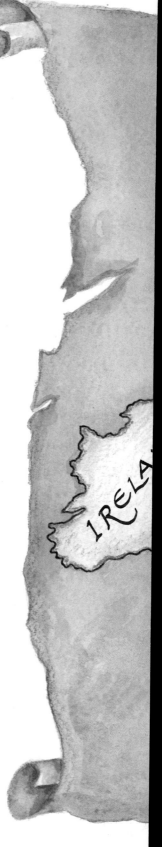

NORWAY

SWEDEN

SCOTLAND

NORTH

NORTHUMBRIA

DENMARK

SEA

Lindisfarne
Bamburgh

Jarrow

York

WALES

MERCIA

EAST
ANGLIA

Athelney

ESSEX
London
KENT

WESSEX

SUSSEX

Hastings

ENGLISH CHANNEL

NORMANDY

Paris

FRANCE

England
in the 8th Century

The **VIKINGS**
are coming!

Alfred the Great

Born 849   Ruled 871 – 899

NOBODY EXPECTED ALFRED TO BECOME the first king of England. And no one guessed he'd end up being called Alfred the Great. He certainly wasn't a great young man. He was shy, had panic attacks, and suffered from a painful illness that was so embarrassing nobody wrote down what it was.

But Alfred's father, Athelwulf, king of Wessex, died. Then so did Alfred's four older brothers, and Alfred was eventually crowned. Not that he inherited a great kingdom – it was surrounded by furious Vikings. Soon all that was left of his West Saxon kingdom was the Isle of Athelney – a tiny piece of Somerset in the middle of a swamp. But it was there that Alfred welded his arguing tribesmen into a fighting force. They overthrew the Vikings who then became Christians, and Alfred began the job that made him great. He created a kingdom with laws which would be fair to everyone – Mercians, Northumbrians, Saxons – even Vikings! Alfred had invented a big idea: that his people weren't just members of a tribe; they were also subjects ruled by the same leader – the king of England!

Alfred the crafty

Young Alfred loved to listen to poems about brave warriors and their heroic deeds. One day, his mother held a competition for her children. Whichever one first learnt to read her book of Saxon poetry could keep it. Alfred was the youngest. He was only four, but he learnt the poems by heart, pretended he could read them and won the prize.

Alfred the cunning

One night he entered the Vikings' camp disguised as a wandering musician, and stole their battle plans from under their noses.

Alfred the kind

There is a legend that when Alfred was hiding from the Vikings, he took shelter in a peasant woman's hut. She didn't recognise him, and told him he could stay if he looked after her cakes, which were cooking on the fire. He sat there thinking over his battle plans, and forgot what he was supposed to be doing. The woman returned to find her hut full of smoke, and drove Alfred out in a fury. At that moment her husband arrived, recognised the king, and the two peasants dropped to their knees, terrified that they'd be punished. Instead Alfred lifted them to their feet and said how sorry he was for burning the cakes.

Alfred's enemy and Alfred's friend

Guthrum was a great Viking leader who overran most of England and drove Alfred back into the Isle of Athelney. But Alfred rallied his troops and captured Guthrum who decided to turn his back on the ancient Viking gods. He allowed Alfred's priests to lead him round the countryside dressed in white with his hands tied up as a symbol that the Christian god was now his master. Although Alfred and Guthrum still fought each other occasionally, they agreed to divide England between them, and when fresh Viking invaders arrived from Denmark, Guthrum fought on Alfred's side.

The big ships sail

The Vikings came by sea. So Alfred decided to beat the invaders at their own game. He built bigger ships – twice as long as the enemy's – with sixty oars or more.

WIDER AND LONGER

Alfred, England and the English

How did England get its name? Alfred was an Anglo-Saxon, his united tribes were called the 'Angles', which after a while became 'English'; and Alfred called his kingdom 'Anglecynn', which meant 'land of the English people'. Although we now know that Alfred's creation was here to stay, it was by no means certain at the time and often it seemed the country would fall apart again.

Alfred the teacher

Hardly anyone in Alfred's time could read or write. Alfred realised this didn't make a strong country – what was the use of having good laws and brilliant battle plans if no one could read them? Something needed to be done. So he brought teachers from other countries to his court, started schools for both boys and girls, and began building up the libraries that had been destroyed by the Vikings – he even wrote some books himself.

Alfred the Great

King Alfred began with a tiny little kingdom in the middle of a swamp. By the time he died he was the ruler of a great country. If he hadn't been such a good king, England could have ended up as part of Denmark, and today the English might all speak Danish. On his death at around age fifty his son Edward became king. Alfred had trained him well.

Meanwhile

• 890 *English horses get their first horseshoes*
• 890 *Alfred orders a written history of England to be begun - the Anglo-Saxon Chronicle*

Edward the Elder

Born 870 Ruled 899 – 924

Edward the Elder was a GREAT soldier who carried on the work started by his father. Under his rule England got bigger and stronger and better organised. It's rather unfair that his subjects didn't call him Edward the Elder the Great – but that would have been a bit of a mouthful.

Sister in arms

Edward didn't triumph alone. His sister Aethelflaed, called 'the Lady of the Mercians', was powerful and clever and more than a match for the Vikings. She organised the building of fortified towns, led battles, and even managed to win some land from the Vikings.

A small hiccup called Elfweard

Born 891 Ruled 924

On Edward's death his second son, Elfweard, was crowned but died two weeks later. No one knows why. His elder brother, Athelstan, then became king. Curious people might have wondered if Athelstan had something to do with his brother's death – but he was a fierce warrior and no one dared ask him.

Athelstan

Born 894 Ruled 924 – 939

Athelstan was yet another GREAT king. He was clever. He was religious. He never lost a battle. By now all his subjects thought this new invention called 'the king of England' was an extremely good idea. The only problem was that Athelstan never married. So when he died, his half-brother, Edmund, took the job.

A kind little boy

King Alfred was very fond of his grandson, Athelstan, because when the old king was ill, little Athelstan would chatter to him and wipe the cold sweat from his forehead.

A fierce young man

In 937 the Vikings joined with the Welsh and Scots to invade England. Athelstan beat them at the Battle of Brunanburh. So many men were killed that the soil turned dark red.

Meanwhile

• 933 Normandy in France became a small independent state ruled by a duke. These dukes were very important to the story of England's kings and queens. Why? Because a hundred years later one of them invaded England and conquered the whole country.

Edmund the First

Born 921 Ruled 939 – 946

Edmund might have been GREAT but he was killed before he had the chance to be. He made a good start. Some parts of England were still ruled by Vikings and Edmund managed to win back some land from them and make friends with the Danish settlers who had been under their rule. But one day he saw a well-known robber in his feasting hall. Edmund was so angry he grabbed the robber by the hair and dragged him out the door. Unfortunately for Edmund, the robber was even angrier. He drew a knife and killed the king.

Edred

Born 924 Ruled 946 – 955

Edred was Edmund's younger brother. He lost some land to the Norsemen, then won it back again by driving out and killing the fearsome Norse king Eric Bloodaxe.

Edred may have been a quite a good ruler, but he had a disgusting habit: he couldn't chew his food properly and let it dribble down his chin. This made his dinner guests feel sick. He ruled for nine years, although to his dinner guests it must have seemed like ninety! When he died his nephew Edwig became king and he was absolutely useless.

Edwig

Born 942 Ruled 955 – 959

There is a legend that at a banquet on the day he was crowned, fourteen-year-old Edwig sneaked off and was caught by a famous bishop called Dunstan chatting up a young girl *and* her mother. Dunstan was furious. He hadn't even finished his pudding first! The following year Edwig married the girl and banned Dunstan from his court. A lot of people disapproved of Edwig, and it's not hard to see why. He died of a mysterious illness when he was seventeen. He was followed by his brother, Edgar.

Edgar the Peaceful

Born 944 Ruled 959 – 975

Edgar finished off the job his great-grandfather Alfred had begun. Under him and Archbishop Dunstan, England became truly one nation and everyone accepted Edgar as their rightful king. The country was now rich, law-abiding and peaceful. Viking pirates stayed away from its shores, and the church had all the power it wanted. But then Edgar died and things went downhill fast.

Edgar beats the wolves

Wild wolves were a problem in Edgar's time. But he hunted a great many down and the rest fled to Wales. He then ordered the Welsh princes to send him 300 wolves' heads a year and soon there were virtually none left.

So who invented the coronation?

When Bishop Dunstan became an archbishop he came up with a plan. Many people worshipped the Viking gods and that made him furious. He wanted Christianity to become England's only religion. He decided the best person to make sure this happened was the king. He created a big show called the coronation. On the day each new king was crowned, he had to promise to be good and to protect the Christian religion. The first big coronation was for Edgar. Not only was he crowned, but so was his wife, Elfrida, who became queen of England. Their son Edward would be the next king.

Edward the Martyr

Born 963 Ruled 975 – 978

Edward was crowned when he was twelve, but he was dead by the time he was fifteen. He went to stay at his stepmother's castle and was murdered there. His stepmother, Elfrida, swore she had nothing to do with it, but her revolting son Ethelred was the new king and she became the most powerful woman in England. So whatever anyone thought, they weren't about to argue with her!

Blue tooth

But Ethelred was in for some big trouble. During Edward's reign, the ferocious Viking king Harold Bluetooth trained up a great army of fearsome warriors more savage and bloodthirsty than any that had come before. And by the time Ethelred became king, they were looking for some heads on which to try out their new battle-axes.

Ethelred the Unready

Born 968 Ruled 978 — 1016

It may not be fair to judge someone who lived over a thousand years ago, but some people deserve it. For instance, take Ethelred. He totally failed to protect England from the ferocious new Vikings. Time after time, he would bribe them to go back to Denmark. They would leave loaded with English money, only to sail back soon after to ask for more. He was also a terrible judge of character. Throughout his reign he promoted people who were no good at their jobs, or were traitors, or were both. The few times he did have good people working for him, he had them tortured or murdered. Ethelred was suspicious and cruel, and eventually decided to massacre every Viking who lived in England. He may have thought this would make the country safer but it didn't. It made things worse.

The Vikings in Denmark were furious and they became absolutely determined to overthrow him. So by the time he died, England was bankrupt, defeated and occupied by its enemies. Ethelred may have loved his mother, he may have been kind to his horse, but as a king he was absolutely dreadful.

A useless old king

Ethelred ruled England for thirty-eight years. In 1013 he ran away to France because he was so frightened of the Vikings. But the English nobles said he could come back and be king again as long as he promised to be better behaved. He agreed, returned and then murdered his top general's brother. Yes, he was as cruel and as useless as before.

Meanwhile

• 981 The Viking Eric the Red discovers Greenland

A joke for a name

Ethelred's name is a joke. In old English 'Ethelred' means 'good advice', and 'un-red' means 'bad advice'. So Ethelred's name was really 'Good Advice-Bad Advice'.

Today we call him Ethelred the Unready – which is fair enough because he was that as well!

Edmund Ironside

Born 993 Ruled 1016

With Ethelred dead, the English crowned his son Edmund, but the Vikings wanted the Danish king, Cnut, to be king. For a year the Vikings and the English fought each other. Edmund was tough – that's why he was called Ironside – and he won some impressive victories, but his army lost at the Battle of Ashingdon. Edmund was hurt and was forced to share his kingdom with Cnut. A month later Edmund died – perhaps of his wounds – so maybe Ironside wasn't such a good name for him after all.

King Cnut

Born 995   Ruled 1016 — 1035

CNUT WAS THE SON OF A VIKING KING. Before he came to England he was a ferocious, bloodthirsty warrior, a 'wild man'. When he became king he realised it would be sensible to calm down a bit and try to appear more regal. He made some good laws, built some monasteries and divided England up into four great earldoms, which everyone seemed to think was a good idea. However, Cnut had one big problem. He was also king of Denmark and Norway. Whenever he concentrated on one kingdom, the other two rebelled. But even if he had a hard time keeping his nations under control, most people thought he was wise.

Cnut became the most powerful king in western Europe and there was no shortage of smarmy followers keen to win his favour. Pretty soon he was fed up with his nobles saying how great he was. When one of them claimed Cnut was so wonderful even the sea would obey him, it was the last straw. Cnut sat in his throne on the beach and ordered the sea to go back. It didn't, of course, and he got soaking wet. No one knows whether this story is true, but it does show that Cnut was wise enough not to pretend that he possessed superpowers.

Cnut the Viking

Cnut was the first king of England for almost one hundred and fifty years who wasn't related to Alfred the Great. He wasn't even English. So if an Englishman had asked Cnut to spare his life, Cnut wouldn't have known what he was talking about because he didn't speak English.

For the next two hundred and fifty years nearly all of England's kings would be French or Danish and very few of them would understand what their subjects were saying. These kings were soldiers. Most of them were rough men and many were cruel, but under their leadership England became very powerful. That's no excuse for bullying, but it is a fact.

Cnut/Canute

Some English history writers had a problem with the fact that Cnut was a Viking. They wanted people to think that all the kings before William the Conqueror were Englishmen. So they changed Cnut's name to Canute, which they thought sounded a bit more English. To this day the Danes call him Cnut the Great, but the English don't even call him Cnut, let alone Cnut the Great.

Berserk berserkers

The most fearsome Vikings were the berserkers (which means bearskin in Danish), who would work themselves up into a frenzy of rage and fight wearing animal skins. They believed that while fighting they became wolves or bears and couldn't be harmed. They were allowed to challenge anyone to a duel to the death and it wasn't wise to refuse! To help his new, more civilised image Cnut decided to ban these duels and made berserking illegal!

Peeping Tom and the Lady

There is a legend that one of Cnut's earls, Lord Leofric, promised the people of Coventry that he would reduce their taxes if his wife, Lady Godiva, agreed to ride naked through the city. Everyone promised to stay indoors and shut their eyes. They all kept their promise except for a little boy called Tom. He peeped through a hole in the shutter of his window and was so surprised by the sight of a nude woman riding a horse that he went blind!

The not-always-wise king

Cnut married King Ethelred's widow, Emma, which was very wise because it stopped her supporters fighting him. They had a son called Hardicnut, and Cnut promised Emma that he would be the next king. This was not very wise because he already had two sons by his first wife, and both wanted the crown for themselves. Clearly there would be some serious squabbling soon.

Harold
(Called Harefoot because he was such a fast runner)

Born 1015 Ruled 1037 – 1040

When Cnut died, his son Hardicnut couldn't come to England to pick up the crown because he was too busy fighting in Denmark. So his half-brother, Harold Harefoot, very kindly ran the country for him for two years, then crowned himself king and threw Hardicnut's mother out of the country. Hardicnut was furious and set sail for England. But before he got there, Harold died, saving Hardicnut the bother of killing him.

Hardicnut

Born 1017 Ruled 1040 – 1042

Hardicnut hated Harold Harefoot even after he was dead. The first thing he did on reaching England was to rip open his brother's grave and hurl his body into a bog. Two years after he was crowned he had a fit after drinking too much at a wedding. He was clearly a very excitable person!

Edward the Confessor

Born 1002 Ruled 1042 – 1066

Edward was yet another half-brother of Harold Harefoot. He was tall and religious and looked like people thought kings should look. But looks aren't everything. He was actually very weak and couldn't stand up to his bossy nobles. The bossiest was Godwin, who was always telling him what to do. Edward tried fighting him. He tried accusing him of murder. He tried throwing him out of the country. But Godwin wouldn't keep quiet. Then Godwin died. Edward must have been over the moon with relief. But Godwin had a son called Harold Godwinson who was even bossier. Edward busied himself by building a huge new abbey at Westminster. It was finished in 1065. This was fortunate for Edward as he died in 1066 – just in time to be buried in his new church.

What's in a name?

As he got older, Edward became more and more religious and people began to believe he could perform miracles. A hundred years after he died he was made a saint and given the name Edward the Confessor.

Never trust a king's promise

Promise number one: Edward promised his distant French cousin William of Normandy that when he died he could be king.

Promise number two: Edward promised Harold Godwinson that when he died *he* could be king.

This meant there was big trouble brewing!

Harold the Second

Born 1020   Ruled 1066

SINCE ALFRED THE GREAT'S TIME, whenever a king died, the crown passed to his son, brother or some other member of his family. Harold Godwinson stopped all this. When Edward died Harold took over. He wasn't a relative. He wasn't a Viking invader like Cnut. He became king simply because he'd been promised the throne by Edward the Confessor and was supported by most of England's nobles.

In September 1066, the Viking king Hardrada invaded the north with a big army. Harold's soldiers marched 250 miles to meet it. As soon as they'd beaten it, William of Normandy's army sailed from France and landed in the south. So Harold's men had to march 250 miles back south again for a second battle. By the time the two sides met at Hastings, Harold's army was totally worn out. Nonetheless, the night before the battle, the Saxons sang and danced, and the Normans prayed – at least that's what the Normans said afterwards. The battle started at daybreak. Both armies fought bravely, but eventually Harold was killed. Now the Normans ruled England, and some big changes were about to be made!

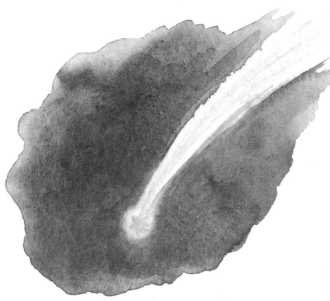

Big boast

The Viking king Hardrada once asked Harold how much of England the king would give him . Harold's reply became famous. He said, 'I'll give you six feet. No, seven feet, as you are a bit taller than most men.' Hardrada was killed fighting Harold's army and his grave was, in fact, seven foot long.

The comet

In April 1066 a comet was seen in the sky above England. A few months later, King Harold was dead and a new, ruthless king sat on the throne of England. It's not hard to see why people believed the comet had been a sign of the disaster to come!

The hoar apple tree

When Harold heard that William had landed, he had a big decision to make. He could wait to build up a new army or launch a surprise attack with the troops he already had. He sent a message to his supporters in the south to join him and his army at a famous landmark near Hastings called 'the hoar apple tree'. From there, he thought he'd be able to surprise William. But things went horribly wrong. The apple tree was so close to William's camp that the Norman soldiers could see Harold's army gathering and prepared for battle. Harold's plan had completely backfired.

An ill wind

In order to invade England, William built a great fleet of ships to carry all the swords, armour, weapons and even horses for the knights. When the ships were ready they were dragged down to the beach. Then the Norman soldiers waited for a strong southerly wind to speed them to England. They were out of luck. For a month the wind blew from the north, which would have slowed their journey and made them easy prey for an English attack. But at the very time Harold was in the north of England celebrating his victory over Hardrada the wind changed. William's fleet was soon racing across the channel, under cover of night, to land unchallenged on England's southern shores.

Harold's eyeful?

Most people think that Harold was killed by an arrow in the eye. This is because on the Bayeux Tapestry the first word of the caption 'Harold is killed' is next to a soldier pulling an arrow out of his eye. But if you look at the whole scene, it seems as if Harold is a different soldier being hacked down by a sword.

William the Conqueror

Born 1028   Ruled 1066 – 1087

HAVING BEATEN HAROLD AT the Battle of Hastings, William of Normandy rode to London, looting and pillaging on the way. Then he gave himself a magnificent coronation at Westminster Abbey on Christmas Day. He was now King William the First and England was ruled by Frenchmen!

William was crude, shrewd and wore his crown a lot to show who was boss. He was full of energy, and determined that the French should have the best of everything. The English lords and churchmen were sacked and French nobles were given their jobs. Many ordinary English people rebelled or rioted. But they didn't stand a chance. William built castles all over the land, filled them with fierce soldiers and ordered them to burn people's land and belongings. There was so much hunger, misery and death that people just gave up.

England's new rulers spoke a foreign language, were fearsome fighters and ruthless about collecting taxes. People hated them, but there was nothing they could do about it.

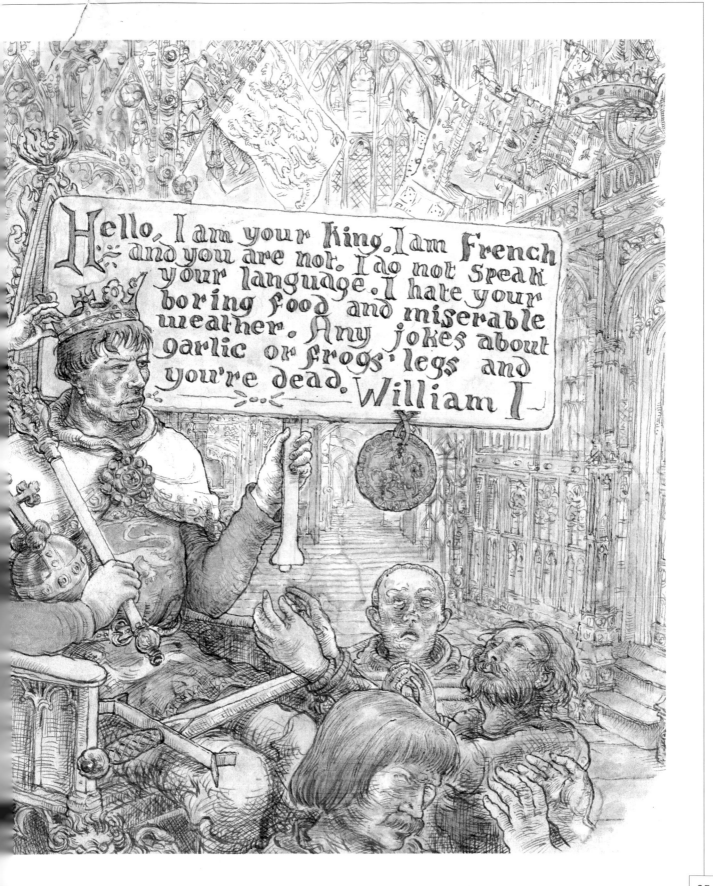

Still standing

Two castles William built to terrify the people of southeast England are still there today – the Tower of London and Windsor Castle. But nowadays people are more frightened of the heavy traffic than of the castles!

The Book of Doom

William didn't do all the conquering on his own. He brought over several friends and relations from France to help him. One of the cleverest was Archbishop Lanfranc. He sent Normans all over England to find out who owned every castle, every house, every cottage, even every pig and wrote it all down in a huge book. From this they worked out how much everyone must pay in taxes. People hated this book. They thought it was as dreadful as the day of doom when the world would end. So they called it the Domesday Book.

Women's unliberation

Until William's time, women had been more or less equal with men. But the Normans changed all that. They decided that men were the superior sex and from now on young women must obey their fathers, married women must obey their husbands and only rich widows could have a say in anything.

The New Forest

King William's hobby was hunting. He already had sixty-eight royal forests, but still wanted a bigger one. So he flattened 150 square miles of Hampshire, planted trees, brought in some deer and called his creation the New Forest. It's still called the New Forest today, even though it's now over 900 years old.

A clumsy horse

As well as being king of England, William still ruled Normandy. In 1087 he went to war with the French king and threatened to set the whole of France ablaze. But while his men were lighting fires, William's horse stumbled, throwing him painfully against the pommel of his saddle. His injuries were so bad that he died a few weeks later. He was buried in France, but his tomb was broken into during the French Revolution 500 years later and his bones scattered.

William had three sons. The eldest, Robert, became Duke of Normandy and the middle one, William Rufus, inherited the English throne. The youngest, Henry, got 5,000 pounds in silver but no royal title at all – but that was soon to change!

William Rufus

Born 1056 Ruled 1087 – 1100

Some people say redheads have fiery tempers and like to get their own way. Redheads get angry about this, but it was certainly true of William's son, William Rufus, who was even more ferocious than his father. Rufus means red, and William Rufus had ginger hair and a terrible temper. His nobles were terrified of him. He loved being in the midst of battle and spent most of his reign trying to win Normandy from his brother Robert. He was killed by an arrow while out hunting in his dad's new forest. Surprisingly, everyone seemed to think it was an accident.

Don't believe what you read until you know who wrote it

Despite his temper tantrums, William Rufus did a good job of being king. He won lots of battles, was clever and worked hard. But the history books of the time tell us he was appalling – a dreadful king, wicked, sinful, greedy and bullying. Why do they say this? Because William Rufus hated churchmen. He may not even have believed in God, and the Church never forgave him. And guess who wrote the history books? The churchmen!

Henry the First

Born 1068 Ruled 1100 – 1135

By a stroke of luck (or was it?) King William's brother Henry was also hunting in the New Forest on the day of the accident. The new king should have been his older brother, Robert, but Henry rushed to Winchester to seize the treasury and then on to Westminster to have himself crowned before anyone had the chance to argue.

Like his brother Rufus and his father, William the Conqueror, Henry the First was tough, sturdy and good at being king. He even married an Englishwoman, Matilda, great-granddaughter of King Edmund Ironside, and that pleased his subjects very much. The English kingdom was going from strength to strength, getting bigger, richer and safer for its subjects.

Henry loved having children – the more the merrier. He had twenty-eight in all, although their mothers tended to be his girlfriends and Queen Matilda was mother to only two. After his darling son was drowned when the royal boat, *The White Ship*, sank in the English Channel, Henry promised the throne to his daughter, also called Matilda. But the English lords didn't like the idea of a female monarch, and they certainly didn't like Matilda.

A fishy death

Henry died after eating too many lampreys too quickly. Lampreys are tiny eels with round mouths that they use as suckers. Why he ate one, let alone too many, is hard to imagine!

Stephen

Born 1096 Ruled 1135 – 1154

and Matilda – Lady of the English

Born 1104

Stephen was Matilda's cousin. In those days, most people thought girls were weak and silly and wouldn't know how to fight. But Matilda was strong and brave and she certainly did know how to fight. While Matilda was trying to get the nobles to let her be queen, Stephen got himself made king behind her back. This started years of chaos as the two fought each other over who should be ruler. On one occasion Stephen's army trapped Matilda in Oxford Castle and kept her under siege. On a deathly cold winter night, Matilda dressed herself in white clothes so she wouldn't be seen against the snow, then bravely escaped across the frozen River Thames to safety.

On another occasion, Matilda defeated Stephen, went to London and was about to be made queen. But she was so rude and proud that the Londoners rose up and drove her out. So the war dragged on. In the end, Matilda gave up and Stephen, who had no heir, promised to let her son Henry be the next king. It was a pity they hadn't thought of that in the first place!

Meanwhile, however, the barons had been getting stronger, doing as they liked, bullying and torturing the peasants. Would the king cope with them, or would there be even more trouble?

Henry the Second

Born 1133   Ruled 1154 – 1189

HENRY THE SECOND WAS BIG TROUBLE! He was short and stocky with a neck like a bull and blazing grey eyes that flashed about in a fiery face. His huge head was topped with a short crop of vivid red hair and when he was in a rage he would throw himself on the floor and gnash the rushes that covered it in his teeth. But he was also brilliantly clever. In fact, he was a bit of a genius.

His reign started well. He got his barons under control and made the English Empire bigger and stronger. He set up new, fairer law courts and money rolled into the royal treasure chest. The country hadn't been so well ruled for years. But Henry had a terrible temper, and tended to take it out on his family. He didn't go in for little quarrels about what time the children should go to bed. These were full-scale blazing rows that often left people without their lands, and sometimes without their heads. He was horrible to his beautiful, clever wife, Eleanor, who was then horrible back to him. He was just as horrible to his children, so they rebelled against him. The country was crumbling again, simply because the king's family life was such a mess.

Henry's temper
(or, kings don't always mean what they say)

Henry had a big row with his friend Thomas à Becket, the Archbishop of Canterbury. One day, in a moment of irritation, Henry snapped the words, 'Will no one rid me of this turbulent priest?' Four knights overheard, and thought this meant the king would be pleased if they killed Thomas for him. They rode to Canterbury and murdered Thomas on the altar steps. Henry was very shocked. He hadn't really meant what he'd said. He ordered a huge tomb to be built for his friend, and, throwing himself on the floor in front of it, allowed himself to be flogged by monks by way of punishment.

Henry's Queen Eleanor

Eleanor was just as wilful as her husband. When she met Henry she was already married to King Louis of France. But she was so taken with the new young English king that she decided she would rather be married to him. So she divorced her first husband, married Henry and became queen of England. She was strong, beautiful and clever. A bit too clever, thought Henry. He became worried she would challenge his power, so he put her under house arrest and got himself a docile, adoring girlfriend instead.

Three devil kings

People said that Henry came from the devil and to the devil he would return. They also said he couldn't help fighting his sons because the blood of the devil ran in their veins too. Two of them, Richard and John, became kings of England, so if people were right England had three devil kings.

Henry Plantagenet

Henry's father, Geoffrey, was French. He was famous for wearing a piece of broom in his hat. This doesn't mean he had stiff bristles tickling his forehead or a big pole dangling down his back. Broom is a plant with yellow flowers. The French word for broom is *genet*, so Geoffrey was known as Plantagenet. It may be rather difficult to spell, but it's an unusual nickname and it stuck. Geoffrey's whole family became known as the Plantagenets, including Henry and his children. The Plantagenet family now replaced the Normans as rulers of England, just as one hundred years before, the Normans had replaced the Saxons.

Richard
the Lionheart

Born 1157   Ruled 1189 – 1199

WHEN HENRY DIED, HIS ELDEST living son, Richard, became king. Nearly everyone has heard of Richard the Lionheart. He was tall, majestic, gifted and brave. What a fine and noble English king! But was he really? The truth is he was also vengeful, cruel and big-headed and spent only six months of his entire reign in England.

Shortly after being crowned, Richard decided to become a crusader. This meant sailing across the sea to Palestine to join Christian armies fighting the Muslims who lived there. He was very good at this and stayed away a long time. When he finally decided to return home he was kidnapped. The English paid a huge ransom so they could get their king back, causing poverty and famine throughout the land. But Richard got bored in England and left for France to do some more slaughtering.

The Crusades

The kings of Europe were all Christians, and were very unhappy that Jerusalem, the city where Jesus died, was occupied by Muslims, followers of Islam. So they sent huge expeditions called Crusades to the faraway country of Palestine to win the city back. But Jerusalem is a holy city for Islam too, and the Muslims were determined not to leave. There were several big Crusades over many years, and a lot of innocent blood was shed, but eventually the Crusaders realised they could never win, so they came back home. Not much good came out of the Crusades except the English learnt about luxury goods such as silks, spices and rice and how to build bigger boats in which to carry them.

Blondel the minstrel

On his way home from Palestine, Richard was captured by the Duke of Austria and thrown into prison. No one in England knew where he was. A legend says that a close friend of Richard's, a minstrel called Blondel, toured round the castles of Europe looking for him. One day, high up in his prison tower, the king heard Blondel below singing a song the minstrel had once written for him. Richard bawled out the chorus, and Blondel knew he'd found the right place. He rushed home to tell the English nobles, who happily paid a huge ransom to get their king back. This is a very romantic story, but it's hard to believe that anyone would pay a huge ransom happily, particularly one so huge it brought a whole country to its knees. But that's the sort of story they tended to tell in those days.

Did Robin Hood really exist?

Everyone knows the story of Robin Hood – how he had all his land stolen by the Sheriff of Nottingham when Good King Richard was away fighting the Crusades, and how Robin fled to Sherwood Forest with a band of outlaws called the Merry Men. But is it true? It's certainly true that while Richard was out of the country, his brother John's supporters stole people's land. It's also true that many bandits became outlaws and poached the king's deer in order to live. So even if Robin Hood didn't exist, lots of people like him did.

Fatal arrow

Richard died after he was shot by a cross-bow bolt and his shoulder went mouldy. This famous English king was buried in the French town of Fontevrault, his heart was cut out and presented to the French cathedral at Rouen, and he left his guts to the people of Charroux . . . in France. The new king was his brother John.

Meanwhile

• *1190s Chess and horse racing become popular in England*

King John

Born 1167   Ruled 1199 – 1216

JOHN WAS RICHARD THE LIONHEART'S YOUNGEST BROTHER and being the baby of the family he was horribly spoilt. His brothers were always fighting with the king, but John was too small to take part so he became the apple of his father's eye. Maybe it's not surprising that he grew up to be a cruel, greedy monarch who thought kings should be able to do anything they wanted.

John loved jewels, fine clothes, rich food and getting his own way. He starved his best friend's family to death just because they annoyed him, and upset everyone by having his young nephew Arthur murdered in case he challenged him for the throne. John won a few battles and sorted out some tricky things like the best way to collect taxes, but he wasn't really a very good king. During his reign England lost nearly all its land in France.

John was constantly demanding money from his barons to fight the French. They got so fed up with this that they formed an army and marched on his palace. Finally, at Runnymede, a meadow by the River Thames, the barons forced him to sign an important paper called Magna Carta. This said that from now on, the king had to ask his barons how the country should be run and he couldn't do just as he liked any more. This was good for the country, but it didn't bring back to life any of the people John had killed. The king's final disaster occurred when he tried to cross an estuary on the way from Norfolk to Lincolnshire. He was so impatient, he didn't wait for the tide to go back and some of his jewels, baggage and even members of his household sank in quicksand. When he died a few days later, and his nine-year-old son Henry became king, no one was really sorry.

King John is forced to sign Magna Carta

Henry the Third

Born 1207 Ruled 1216 — 1272

Henry was only nine years old when he became king and that's young to run a raffle, let alone a country! The Plantagenets always wanted to have their own way, and Henry was a Plantagenet through and through. This didn't create too many problems to start with because, while he was a boy, some fairly sensible nobles looked after the kingdom for him. Things started to go wrong when he turned twenty-one. He sacked his nobles and relied instead on his friends, most of whom hadn't the faintest idea how to run a country. He tried to recapture the land lost by his father, but he wasn't a soldier and failed miserably. He was too proud to listen to good advice, had temper tantrums and spent a fortune on glorifying his palaces.

Henry believed that kings were holy and should be worshipped like saints. He didn't think that any of England's churches were grand enough for kings to be crowned or buried in. So he ordered Westminster Abbey to be rebuilt in the style of a magnificent

palace and then dug up his father, King John, and Edward the Confessor, and had them reburied in expensive new tombs. From then on nearly all of England's kings and queens were crowned and buried at the abbey.

And although he shouted a lot, deep down he was a coward. He was scared not only of his enemies but also of his son Edward. He was definitely not one of England's better kings.

The first Parliament

Henry's nobles and bishops were so annoyed by Henry's behaviour that they decided to hold a meeting. They invited the knights and big landowners along too, so everyone could have their say. They called this meeting a 'parliament', and from then on Parliament met in order to make rules, to decide how to run the country and, more often than not, to tell the king what they thought of him.

Long live the little king

No one complained when Henry became king, even though he was only a boy. People now accepted that when a king of England died, his oldest son had the right to be the next king. A few doubters were worried that one day the oldest son might be stupid, or mad, or both, and there might be trouble trying to swap him for somebody else. And as things turned out, they were sometimes right!

Meanwhile

• 1206 *Fearsome Mongol warrior Temejin is proclaimed Genghis Khan (Very Mighty Warrior)*
• *During Henry the Third's reign, the scientist Roger Bacon invents eye glasses*
• 1242 *Gunpowder comes to England from the Far East*

Edward the First

(Called Long-Shanks because of his long legs)

Born 1239 Ruled 1272 – 1307

Henry's son, Edward the First, managed to rule England rather well. He was bossy, had the usual Plantagenet temper tantrums and was cruel and violent – even to his own children. But he kept his promises, was brave and energetic and in order to stop revolts from breaking out, built lots of big castles all over the country, many of which are still standing today. He brought in new, fair laws and punished anyone who broke them. He was definitely good at his job, and might have been even better if he hadn't been so ruthless, but at least he was better than his son, Edward the Second.

Edward's big idea

Edward had a grand plan. Being king of England wasn't enough; he wanted to rule Scotland and Wales as well and decided it was time they were conquered. Surprisingly, he was the first English king to attempt this. (Other kings had seemed more interested in French territory than expanding their kingdoms at home.) So did his plan work?

The Welsh princes

Edward went to war with the little states which made up Wales and beat their best warrior, Prince Llywelyn. The Welsh nobles submitted to Edward but said they wanted a new prince who had been born in Wales and didn't speak English. But Edward had a trick up his sleeve. His baby son had been born in Wales and couldn't talk at all, let alone speak English! So one-year-old Edward was presented as their future Prince of Wales. Ever since, the eldest son of the monarch has been the Prince of Wales.

The Scottish kings

The Scots weren't easy to beat. They had their own kings and didn't want an English monarch telling them what to do. Edward won the first battle, and even managed to steal the Stone of Scone, where the Scottish kings were crowned, and take it to London. But the Scots fought back and they started to win! First they were led by a fierce warrior called William Wallace and then, after Wallace was caught and executed, by Robert Bruce, whom they made their king. Edward never gave up, even to the end. He died setting out to fight yet another battle. His servants had been ordered not to bury him but to carry his bones with the army until Scotland was finally defeated. Understandably no one wanted the grizzly job and his son, Edward the Second, had him buried at Westminster Abbey.

Edward loves Eleanor

Edward adored his wife, Eleanor. When she died, he was so heartbroken he ordered magnificent stone crosses to be built at each place her coffin rested on its way to Westminster Abbey. Three of them are still there today.

Edward the Second

Born 1284 Ruled 1307 – 1327

Edward the Second liked parties and feasts but he definitely wasn't a family man. He even spent his wedding night with his handsome male friend Piers Gaveston rather than his wife. This kind of behaviour made him very unpopular at court, and his popularity wasn't helped by his record on the battlefield. He lost to the Scots, the Irish and the French. Eventually his wife, Queen Isabella, and his nobles had had enough of him and they organised a revolt. He was captured, and forced to hand over the crown to his son, Edward the Third. He was imprisoned in Berkeley Castle and then murdered by having a red-hot poker pushed up his bottom. A more unpleasant death it's hard to imagine.

Edward the Third

Born 1312 Ruled 1327 – 1377

Edward the Third hated his mother, Queen Isabella. He was fifteen when his father, King Edward, was murdered, so the queen and her boyfriend, Roger Mortimer, ran the country for him. But as soon as he was old and powerful enough, he had Roger's head cut off and his mother put under house arrest. That's the kind of man he was. He loved fighting and spent a fortune on wars with the French. Of course, it wasn't his money, it belonged to his countrymen, and they got very angry about it. But soon Edward and his son (called the Black Prince because of the black armour he wore) started winning lots of battles, and he became more popular.

Edward loved being king and spent even more money trying to make his court as magnificent as the fairy-tale court of King Arthur. He held fantastic tournaments to train young knights and rebuilt Windsor Castle to stage great festivals there. But when his beloved wife, Philippa, died, he became ill and a bit mad. He retired to live with the wife of one of his knights, Alice Perrer, but she only liked him for what she could get out of him, and pranced around wearing the dead queen's jewels. Slowly all his good work started to fall apart. Then the other love of his life, the Black Prince, died of fever. Edward's friends and courtiers began deserting him in droves, including the grasping Alice who even ripped the rings from his fingers as he lay dying. So however noble a king he may have been when he was young, by that time no one really cared.

The Hundred Years War

King Charles the Fourth of France died without any sons. Edward the Third was his nephew and claimed the throne, but the French chose another relative called Philip instead. Edward gathered an army and invaded France to make himself king. At first the French did well, then Edward won a great

victory at Crécy in 1346. The English kings fought the French for years and years until 1453 when the French finally won. The war is known as the Hundred Years War, although it should really have been called the One Hundred and Twenty-Five Years War, because that's how long it lasted.

The Black Death

In 1348 a terrible new disease hit England. People became sick, coughed up blood, and large black lumps (some the size of apples) appeared under their armpits. Most people who caught the disease died within three days, some died in less than one hour. It was called the Black Death and killed about one third of the population of Europe.

Knights in armour

Edward the Third was very keen on something called chivalry. Some people thought this simply meant that it was all right to kill people as long as you were polite about it, but Edward's court took it very seriously. Knights had to be brave but not cruel, and swear to rescue ladies from danger. Huge tournaments were held in which these knights dressed up, fought each other and showed off like mad.

The Black Prince

The Black Prince (who was also called Edward) was a great fighter, but he treated his enemies with respect. When the French king, John the Good, was held captive in England, the prince didn't have his arch enemy put in chains. Instead, he treated him like an important guest. He stood behind his chair when he ate and when they rode through London, the French king sat on a charger, while the Black Prince trotted along on a little pony.

Richard the Second

Born 1367 Ruled 1377 – 1399

Richard the Second was the Black Prince's son. He was only ten when he was crowned, so his uncle, John of Gaunt, looked after the kingdom for him. Richard's behaviour was appalling. He was rude, boastful, had a violent temper and when he couldn't get his way, he was mean and cruel. Revolting children usually grow out of it but Richard didn't and his nobles wouldn't allow him to run the country even when he became of age. Eventually he did take over, but then the trouble started. He began ordering everyone around and wouldn't listen to good advice. He was very vain and decked himself out in the most ridiculous finery. His fur-trimmed sleeves reached down to the floor, and the

toes of his shoes were so long they had to be fastened to his knees by chains. He wore big gold bows on his legs and covered himself from head to toe in jewels. He must have looked like a walking Christmas tree. To show everyone how important he was he built himself an enormous throne and if anyone caught his eye they were forced to fall to their knees.

As Richard got older he became more and more jealous of his uncle John and even threatened to kill him. Eventually, John's son, Henry Bolingbroke, decided that things were getting out of hand, and led a rebellion against him. He captured Richard and had him murdered. Very few tears were shed.

Richard may have been a rotten king but we have one very important thing to thank him for. It was his idea to use small pieces of cloth to keep his nose clean. Yes, Richard the Second invented the handkerchief!

Henry the Fourth

Born 1366 Ruled 1399 – 1413

Henry's big problem was that not everyone thought it was right for him to be king. Not only had he murdered King Richard the Second, but he wasn't Richard's son or even his grandson, he was just his cousin. So there was no real reason for him to be given the crown, apart from the fact that he wanted it, and he had an army of soldiers with extremely sharp swords to make sure he got it. There was even a rumour that during his coronation a burst of wind blew the crown off his head, which was thought to be a sign that he had no right to be king. Lots of nobles decided to fight against him, and they were helped by the Welsh, the French and the Scots. But finally Henry managed to get Parliament to agree that he was the rightful king. This was a big triumph. It meant the Plantagenets no longer ruled England. Henry's son, Henry the Fifth, would be the next king, and his family, the Lancastrians, were the royal family now.

Burnt at the stake

In Henry's reign, a vicar named William Sautre became the first person in England to be burnt at the stake because of his religious opinions. Many people like Sautre were becoming unhappy with the way the Church was run. They disagreed with its rules, and wanted the Bible translated into English, which the Pope wouldn't allow. Burning these people didn't stop the criticism. It just grew louder. For the next 300 years the problem of how the Church should be run would create more trouble for the kings and queens of England than anything else.

A cat may look at a king

During Henry's reign ordinary people began to make a lot of money as merchants. One of the most famous was Dick Whittington whose ship was called *The Cat*. He had come to London as a poor boy but ended up as rich as some of the nobles and landowners. This is where the story of Dick Whittington and his cat comes from, its moral being that you needn't be a nobleman to make your fortune.

Meanwhile

• 1382 *The Ming Dynasty takes over the whole of China*

Henry the Fifth

Born 1387 Ruled 1413 – 1422

When Henry the Fifth was in his teens he went out drinking night after night, got into fights and had lots of girlfriends. But if anyone thought he would keep this up when he was king, they were wrong. He was ruthless, ambitious and very serious. He wanted more than a kingdom. He wanted an empire. He crushed his enemies at home, then set sail for France. Once there he won the great Battle of Agincourt. Although he hardly ever returned to England, his subjects assumed he must be a very good king because he won so many battles. Henry never achieved his ambition of ruling both England and France because he died of dysentery when he was only thirty-five. Had he lived longer he might have become the greatest king England has ever known. On the other hand he might have started losing, and become really unpopular. We'll never know. When you're a successful king, dying young can be a big plus.

Henry the Sixth

Born 1421 Ruled 1422 – 1461

To become king when you are nine months old isn't just strange, it's completely ridiculous. When Henry the Sixth came to the throne he couldn't even put his own crown on. How was he supposed to give orders if all he could do was gurgle? But he was Henry the Fifth's son, and even if he wasn't potty-trained, everyone agreed they wanted the rightful heir on the throne, because this would stop the nobles squabbling about which of them should be the next ruler. Henry grew up to be very serious and religious. He was so angry one Christmas when one of his lords brought a group of ladies with bare bosoms to dance before him that he turned his back and stormed out of the room. Not only was he prudish, he was squeamish as well and often stopped people being executed or tortured because he couldn't stand the sight of blood.

He was a kind man whose ambition was to be just as great as the great King Alfred, but you need more than kindness to be great. He chose useless advisors, never led his troops into battle and lost all the lands his father had won in France. To make matters worse, he began having fits of madness and no longer seemed to care about running the country. England began falling apart again. Someone had to do something so along came cousin Edward and . . .

The Wars of the Roses

The Wars of the Roses was not, as it sounds, a battle of flowers. Edward of York decided he would make a better king than his cousin Henry. He also thought he had a stronger claim to the throne. He was descended from Edward the Third's third son, whereas Henry was only descended from his fourth. (This may not seem very important, but to kings and queens this kind of thing matters hugely.) So a war broke out between Henry's family, the Lancasters, whose badge was a red rose and Edward's family, the Yorks, who wore a white rose. There were several fierce battles, many of them led by Henry's wife, Margaret, who was much tougher and more determined than her rather weak husband. Eventually Edward got the upper hand and entered London in triumph. Henry and Margaret fled to Yorkshire, with Edward hot on their heels. It was here, on a freezing battlefield in a storm of snow and wind, that Henry's army was completely crushed and he and Margaret ran away to hide in Scotland.

The white roses had won and Edward of York was now king of England.

Meanwhile

• 1429 French peasant girl, Joan of Arc, wins back the city of Orléans from the English
• 1440 Henry the Sixth founds Eton College
• 1459 The first tennis courts are built

Edward the Fourth

Born 1442 Ruled 1461 – 1470

Some kings were good at their job and some were bad but Edward the Fourth managed to be both at the same time. He was tall, handsome and vain, drank too much and trusted his friends even when they were double-crossing him. He loved parties and would neglect his kingly duties for weeks on end. He could also be cruel and put to death hundreds of his nobles. But he was a brave general and was very good at making money, enforcing good laws and dealing with foreign countries. Edward's advisors wanted him to marry a French princess, but Edward had fallen head over heels in love with a beautiful young widow called Elizabeth Woodville, who refused to have anything to do with him unless he married her. Edward was so besotted he gave in and made her his queen – but in secret because she wasn't from a very noble family. His advisors were furious, especially when Edward brought all her relations to court and gave them important jobs.

Unfortunately for Edward there were a lot of people who supported the Lancaster family and so didn't want him to be king. Henry the Sixth's wife, Margaret, and some

of the leading English nobles joined forces to put Henry back on the throne. They were too strong for Edward, who was forced to flee to France.

Henry the Sixth's second chance

Ruled again briefly 1470 – 1471

Henry the Sixth was back on the throne again. He'd been pretty useless the first time round, what would he be like now? The answer is – even worse. His nobles lost all faith in him, and within a year Edward had returned from France, defeated him in battle and killed his son, also called Edward. A few days later Henry himself was murdered in the Tower of London, and that, for the moment, was the end of the red roses.

Edward the Fourth's second chance

Ruled again 1471 – 1483

With Henry out of the way, Edward the Fourth really knuckled down and tried to make a good job of his second go as king. He made lots of money through clever schemes and pleased people by not asking them for special taxes. He made friends with the French and Scots, and acted like a king was expected to behave by holding big feasts and wearing his crown a lot. Trade began to flourish and England became rich. But was it too good to last? Yes, because Edward died unexpectedly at the age of forty without making sure things would be safe for his son, twelve-year-old Edward the Fifth.

educated. However, many kings didn't like the idea of ordinary people being able to read because educated people were harder to rule.

Edward the tall

Edward the Fourth's tomb was opened up in 1789. His skeleton was found to be 6' 3" long. He was the tallest king of England ever.

Cutting letters on a tree

At the time of the Wars of the Roses, a Dutchman called John Geinsfleish was cutting out letters in the bark of a tree when it occurred to him that he could dip the cutouts in ink and make an impression of the letters on a piece of paper. Some years later in Germany, Johannes Gutenberg took this brilliant inspiration a step further by fixing metal letters to wooden blocks to make moveable type – and printing was invented! Printing meant cheaper books, and cheaper books meant more people could become

Edward the Fifth

Born 1470 Ruled 1483

Edward the Fifth was twelve when his father died. By and large boy-kings hadn't turned into very good man-kings, so would Edward the Fifth be different? He never had the chance to find out. His uncle Richard was made his guardian. Richard locked Edward and his little brother in the Tower of London, and three months later the two boys were murdered. Being a boy-king certainly wasn't easy.

Meanwhile

- *1476 William Caxton prints the first book in English*
- *1481 Bristol sailors discover Newfoundland*

Richard the Third

Born 1452   Ruled 1483 – 1485

IF THERE WAS A COMPETITION FOR unpopular kings, Richard the Third would win hands down.

Compared to him, even bad King John seems like a gentleman! Yet Richard was very talented; he was clever, brave in battle and other kings were impressed by him. But he made one big mistake. On the death of his brother, Edward the Fourth, Richard became guardian to his two nephews, Edward the Fifth, the new young king, and his little brother, Richard. But instead of looking after the two princes, he had them murdered! This upset everyone. (Even though there was no proof of his guilt, the evidence against him was very strong and most people believe he was to blame.) It was also thought that he murdered Edward the Fourth's chamberlain and the previous queen's brother, but people weren't so bothered about that.

Richard tried hard to make his subjects like him. He promised he wouldn't raise their taxes, and told them that from now on, the laws of the land would be fair to everyone, but people didn't care. They just couldn't forget those two little boys.

The Battle of Bosworth

Richard's only real rival for the throne was a distant cousin called Henry Tudor who had been banished to France. But two years after Richard was crowned, Henry landed in Wales with a small army. People rallied to him. There was a battle at Bosworth Field in Leicestershire. Richard fought bravely but was killed. In fact most of the old nobles from the families of York and Lancaster had wiped each other out by now. The Wars of the Roses was over. A new family ruled England: the Tudors.

What a swap!

There is a legend that during the battle Richard's horse was killed under him and, as it's very difficult to do battle on foot, he offered to swap the whole of England for another mount. 'A horse! A horse!' he cried. 'My kingdom for a horse!' Unfortunately for him, no one seems to have heard.

Richard the hunchback

William Shakespeare wrote a famous play about Richard the Third in which the king is a villain with a withered arm and a hunched back. In fact he is often known as Richard Crookback. But although it's true his shoulders were a bit uneven there is no reason to think he really had a twisted body. The Tudors hated Richard and wanted everyone to think badly of him – and who did Shakespeare write his play for? The Tudor queen Elizabeth the First.

Dead and disrespected

Kings, even really bad ones, were usually treated with honour once they were dead. But not Richard the Third. The clothes were ripped from his body. He was trussed up like a sheep, tied to a horse and taken to a remote church to be buried. A few years later his grave was smashed up and his remains were thrown away, never to be found again.

Henry the Seventh

Born 1457 Ruled 1485 – 1509

Henry the Seventh told everyone that he was the true heir to the throne and that God had decided he should be king. Whether God had any opinion on the subject or not we'll never know, but Henry's claim to be the rightful heir was not very good. He was the son of a woman who was the great-granddaughter by his third marriage of a man who was the fourth son of Edward the Third. Not only is this very complicated, but it also made him a very, very, very distant relative of the kings of England. But Henry was smart. Shortly after he was crowned, he married Elizabeth of the House of York and that made the Yorkists happy. Now Henry seemed almost as royal as they were. He started running the country like a business. He had lots of schemes for making money and the gold poured in, so most other people were happy too. He chose clever, loyal men to help him and turned England into a kingdom that was much more modern than most of Europe. He may not be the most famous king of England but he was certainly one of the best. Soon everyone forgot that he had almost no right to be king at all.

Henry's great love

Even though Henry only married his wife, Elizabeth, because she came from a royal family, and he hadn't even met her when they got engaged, he fell passionately in love with her. When she died he was heart-broken. He was so sad he wouldn't let anyone come near him. Then he cheered up and advertised for a new wife, but he died before anyone could reply.

The two pretenders

Because Edward's claim to the throne was not very strong, there were plenty of people willing to try to take it from him. The strangest were two ordinary countrymen Lambert Simnel and Perkin Warbeck. Perkin pretended to be the murdered Edward the Fifth – managing to persuade some people that the young king hadn't really died in the Tower. Lambert pretended to be the nephew of King Edward the Fourth. They must have been quite good actors because first Lambert was actually crowned in Ireland, and then Perkin won the support of the king of France and led an invasion. Both met sad ends. Lambert was captured and forced to work as a skivvy in the royal kitchens, and Perkin was imprisoned in the Tower and then hanged while trying to escape.

Favourites

Henry the Seventh's eldest son and heir to the throne was named Arthur after the legendary king of Round Table fame. When he died, aged only fifteen, Henry was distraught. The next in line was his second son, Henry, but his dad didn't seem to think he was made of the right stuff to be king. Nonetheless, little Henry was determined to prove his father wrong, and become the most famous English king of England ever!

Meanwhile

• 1492 *Christopher Columbus discovers the West Indies*
• 1498 *Christopher Columbus discovers America*
• 1504 *Leonardo da Vinci paints the portrait known as the Mona Lisa*

Henry the Eighth

Born 1491   Ruled 1509 – 1547

HENRY THE EIGHTH WAS A **BIG** king. He had a huge temper, he threw enormous parties and his appetite was gigantic. When he was young, he was handsome, tall and sporty and girls were always falling in love with him. He danced, jousted, wrestled, hunted and was a brilliant tennis player. He also gambled a lot and once bet on whether a man could eat a whole cow! But he was clever and hardworking too. He wrote books, composed songs and built the first modern navy. Unfortunately, Henry was also a bully who wanted to be the most powerful man in the world and he executed anyone who got in his way, including some of his six wives.

But handsome young kings don't always become handsome old kings. In later life, Henry got very fat, bloated and ugly. He was riddled with diseases, had bad breath and smelt horrible. But by the time he died, his brilliance and his appalling behaviour had changed England forever.

Friend or foe?

Henry could be your best friend in the world one minute and your worst enemy the next. Some people even found themselves locked up in the Tower or with their head on the block, just for disagreeing with him!

The Pope

The Pope was the head of the Roman Catholic Church and lived in Rome. He was even more powerful than Henry. When the king was young, the Pope thought he was a good Catholic and gave him the special title 'Defender of the Faith'. But a few years later, Henry asked the Pope if he could divorce his first wife, and got a firm 'No!' for an answer. Henry was so furious he started up his own church, the Church of England, and made himself the head!

Thomas Cromwell

Henry badly needed more money to build new castles and finance his government. His Chancellor, Thomas Cromwell, came up with a devious plan. Now Henry had his own religion, he didn't need the Roman Catholic monasteries any more. So Cromwell ransacked them, stole all their treasure and left them in ruins. The booty was carried back to the king, who was now much richer, but it meant that there were lots of unemployed monks wandering around with nothing to do. Eventually, even clever Cromwell found his head on the block. His crime? Organising an unsuitable marriage for the king!

Thomas Wolsey

Henry had a rich and clever friend called Thomas Wolsey. He was the son of a butcher but was so ambitious he became Lord Chancellor, the Archbishop of York and a cardinal of the Church of Rome. Just one of these jobs would have made him important but all three made him nearly as powerful as the king. For twenty years he helped Henry in every way he could. Then Thomas Wolsey failed to persuade the Pope to agree to Henry's divorce. Henry was furious – he suspected that Thomas hadn't really tried hard enough because he secretly disapproved. He had him arrested for treason, but Thomas died before he could be brought to trial.

Thomas More

After Thomas Wolsey died, Henry made Thomas More Lord Chancellor. He was quiet and humble, but brilliantly clever and devoted to the king. Thomas was also an astrologer and King Henry would sometimes wake him up in the night to go to the top of the castle to study the stars. But Henry's friendship counted for nothing when Thomas More couldn't agree to him being head of the new English church. Henry had him thrown into prison and beheaded.

Henry's delight

Henry often wooed his ladies by playing love songs to them on his lute. He is believed to have written the famous song 'Greensleeves' for Anne Boleyn. Some say this was because she was fond of wearing green; others joke it was because she had the unpleasant habit of wiping her nose on her sleeve.

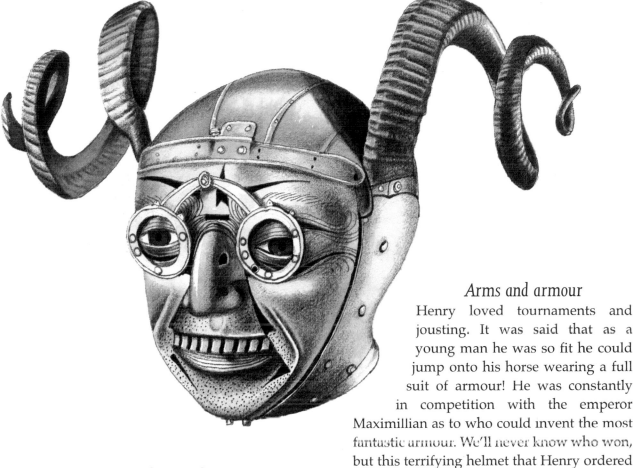

Arms and armour

Henry loved tournaments and jousting. It was said that as a young man he was so fit he could jump onto his horse wearing a full suit of armour! He was constantly in competition with the emperor Maximillian as to who could invent the most fantastic armour. We'll never know who won, but this terrifying helmet that Henry ordered from Germany must have been hard to beat.

What a job!

Henry had a special servant called 'the groom of the stool' whose job was to talk to the king when he was on the toilet!

The king who wouldn't eat his greens

Henry hated fruit and vegetables. His favourite food was meat which he ate for breakfast, lunch, dinner and supper. Not only did this make him ill but he grew to such a monstrous size that he had to be transported up and down stairs in a tram.

The warrior king

As soon as Henry became king he couldn't wait to prove himself in battle, so it wasn't long before he declared war on England's old enemy, France. But although he was a skilled soldier, he wasn't very good at planning battles and only managed to capture a few small towns. He never gave up, even as an old man. During his last attack on France his army could only move at a snail's pace because the king was so enormous and riddled with disease he had to be carried in a special chair. In the end he was only able to win the the seaside town of Boulogne. He died a few years later and so he never did become the great hero of his dreams.

Henry's fabulous feast

Henry's feasts were huge: he once threw a party to impress the king of France. The menu included 30,000 fish, 5,000 chickens and 25,000 litres of beer.

Protesting Protestants

The Roman Catholic Church told people that if they paid a lot of money their sins would be forgiven. During Henry's reign, a young man in Germany, Martin Luther, risked prison and even death by protesting against this. All over Europe people joined the protests. They became known as the 'Protestants', and within a few years they were as powerful as the Catholics.

At first Henry wrote a book against Martin Luther, but in true Henry fashion, he suddenly decided to side with the Protestants when the Pope wouldn't let him get divorced.

He loves me; he loves me not!

Henry is most famous for marrying six times. But it was probably even more dangerous to be his wife than his friend. One day he'd be madly in love with you, and the next he'd be plotting to divorce you or have your head chopped off.

WIFE 1 Catherine of Aragon was the widow of Henry's older brother, Arthur. When they'd been married for eighteen years, Henry fell in love with Anne Boleyn. So Catherine was . . .

Divorced

WIFE 2 Anne Boleyn was one of Catherine's maids of honour. She was pregnant with Henry's daughter Elizabeth when he married her. After three years Henry accused her of sleeping with other men. So Anne was . . .

Beheaded

WIFE 3 Jane Seymour and Henry were married eleven days after Anne Boleyn's execution. They had a son, Edward, but soon after he was born Jane . . .

Died

WIFE 4 Anne of Cleves had never met the king before she married him. She was recommended by Henry's advisor Thomas Cromwell. Henry thought she looked like a horse and from the moment he saw her he couldn't stand her and was furious with Thomas. Anne was . . .

Divorced

WIFE 5 Katherine Howard was the niece of the Duke of Norfolk. After eighteen months, Henry accused her of having slept with another man. He was a very jealous person. Katherine was . . .

Beheaded

WIFE 6 Catherine Parr was a kindly widow. Henry died before she did, so Catherine . . .

Survived

Henry's legacy

When Henry was a little boy he was treated very badly by his father. Then he grew up and had three pale-faced children of his own. But he was even worse to them than his father had been to him. When Henry died, aged fifty-five, his son, Edward, became the new king, and both his daughters, Mary and Elizabeth, would become queens in their turn. The fear they had felt for their cold, angry father affected all of them throughout their reigns.

Meanwhile

- 1517 Coffee arrives in England
- 1520 First bars of chocolate appear in Spain
- 1522 Magellan sets off to sail around the world to prove it is round, but dies on the way
- 1533 Ivan the Terrible becomes king of Russia

Edward the Sixth

Born 1537 Ruled 1547 – 1553

Edward the Sixth was nine years old when he was crowned. He was pale, thin and small but very intelligent – and was nicknamed 'God's imp'. Edward knew what he wanted. He was very interested in the Bible and wanted England to become completely Protestant. His protector, Lord Dudley, encouraged him to make things difficult for the Catholic churches. Then Edward became very ill and it looked as though he was going to die.

This was a big problem for Dudley. The next in line for the throne was Henry the Eighth's daughter Mary and she was a Catholic. If she came to power, Dudley would probably end up without a head. So he hatched a plan to make Lady Jane Grey the next queen. She was Henry the Seventh's great-granddaughter and a Protestant. The beauty of the plan was that she was also married to Dudley's son, Guildford. Edward approved, then died three weeks later. It looked as though the Catholics were in for a very sticky time indeed.

The very, very brief reign of
Lady Jane Grey

Born 1537 Ruled 1553

Things didn't turn out quite like that. Lady Jane Grey was crowned in July 1553 but few people thought she should be queen and she got very little support. Her reign lasted nine days. Then Mary raised an army, took the throne from her, had Dudley's head cut off and flung Lady Jane and her husband into the Tower of London. The following year she had their heads cut off too. By all accounts Lady Jane was a very nice young woman but that didn't count for much in Tudor times.

Mary the First

Born 1516 Ruled 1553 – 1558

Apart from being tiny and very thin, Mary was like her father, Henry. She was musical and could play the lute and spinet. She was clever, could speak several languages and had an iron will. But she also inherited Henry's cruel streak and his pride.

The Tudors had been very good at ruling the country, so people accepted that the next Tudor in line should be their ruler – even if that meant having a woman in charge! Mary became the first English woman to be crowned without a civil war breaking out. But some people worried that a woman on the throne might marry a man the English didn't like – and that he might decide he wanted to be king of England. So they were extremely alarmed when Mary married England's enemy, King Philip of Spain. To make matters worse, Mary started trying to persuade the English back to the Catholic religion. This persuasion involved burning people to death. Her men set fire to over 300 Protestants because they wouldn't stop being Protestants. She became more and more unpopular and when she died there was dancing in the streets. The new monarch was her half-sister, Elizabeth, and a great new age was about to begin.

A chance for sea captains to make some money

King Philip didn't love Mary. He married her so she would help him fight the French. And because she loved him, she agreed. But the war was a disaster for the English. They ended up losing Calais, their one remaining stronghold in France. The English dream of being rulers of France was shattered once and for all. From now on they would have to look further afield for lands to conquer. England's sea captains got their maps out and rubbed their hands with glee. There was a whole world out there across the sea, and the English had some very good ships.

Elizabeth the First

Born 1533   Ruled 1558–1603

QUEEN ELIZABETH THE FIRST WAS BRILLIANT. When she was crowned she was a young woman of twenty-five with bright red hair and piercing grey-black eyes. Although people thought she wouldn't be strong enough to rule a great kingdom, she proved them wrong. Elizabeth said, 'I know I have the body of a weak and feeble woman but I have the heart and stomach of a king, and of a king of England too.'

Elizabeth was the daughter of King Henry the Eighth and Anne Boleyn. She was a great speech writer, a clever politician, and a fine archer and horsewoman. She spoke five languages, including Welsh (which is very difficult to speak – unless you're Welsh!) and, like her father, she could be tough, stubborn and quick-tempered.

Kings, princes and courtiers from all over Europe wanted to marry her but, even though she was a terrible flirt, she stayed single all her life. She knew that if she took a husband he would want to be king and there was no way she would stand for that!

She was extremely vain, and late in life she ordered all the portraits that had been painted of her to be destroyed – except, of course, the ones that made her look beautiful.

The Spanish Armada

The king of Spain wanted to invade England. He put together a huge army of 19,000 men, 8,000 sailors and 130 ships, with another 30,000 soldiers as back-up. Elizabeth's ships were smaller but they were faster and had better guns. When the Spanish anchored off Calais, the English sent in eight blazing boats. The Spanish Armada scattered to avoid the flames and drifted into the open sea where they were attacked. The English sunk seven ships and a storm wrecked even more. It was a disaster for Spain. They lost seventy ships and almost two thirds of their men. The English didn't lose a single ship and only a few hundred men were killed. Not one invader reached the shores of England and Queen Elizabeth became a legend in her own lifetime.

The handsome favourite

Walter Raleigh, a soldier and explorer, was supposed to have pleased the queen by throwing his cloak over a puddle to save the royal shoes getting wet. He was tall, dark and handsome and was one of the queen's favourites at court. But when he got married, Elizabeth imprisoned him in the Tower of London for a while – perhaps she was jealous! Raleigh sent expeditions to set up colonies in America and called one of them Virginia in honour of Elizabeth, who was sometimes called the Virgin Queen.

Were he alive today, many people would like to see him thrown in the Tower again. He helped to introduce a disgusting new habit to the English people – the smoking of a strange new plant called tobacco!

The seafaring favourite

Frances Drake was a daring sea captain, but he was also a pirate. The queen encouraged him to rob the Spanish ships and colonies in the Caribbean and South America. He was the first Englishman to sail around the world and on his return the queen knighted him on the deck of his ship *The Golden Hind.*

Elizabeth and Mary

Elizabeth's court feared that her cousin, Mary Queen of Scots, who was next in line for the throne, was plotting against her. When Mary was forced to flee to England, Elizabeth put her under arrest and kept her shut away for almost twenty years, unable to decide what to do with her. Eventually she had her executed, but felt very sorry afterwards. She cried and cried and couldn't eat or sleep. After all, not only had she ordered the death of a queen, but also of her own cousin!

Fashion queen

Elizabeth had over 3,000 dresses, many embroidered with real gold and jewels. She wore an enormous petticoat called a farthingale and it took her ladies-in-waiting two hours to get her ready in the morning.

Clean (ish) Elizabeth

Elizabeth took a portable bath with her when she travelled from place to place, which meant she was probably a little bit cleaner than most people, who only bathed about three times a year!

Elizabeth on holiday

Elizabeth was famous for travelling around the countryside each summer visiting her subjects. Vast numbers of people went with her, not to mention huge quantities of luggage, clothes and furniture. Why did she go to all this trouble? The answer is partly because it was important that people could see and hear their queen so they would stay loyal to her. But there was another reason. Tudor palaces didn't have running water and got very smelly, particularly in summer. The cleaners needed to get Her Royal Highness out of the way for a few months so they could clean up.

The royal goodbye

Queen Elizabeth the First ruled for forty-four years, kept foreign invaders at bay, encouraged British merchants to make money overseas and strengthened the Church of England. If she had been a king, people would have said she had a triumphant reign, but they were absolutely amazed that a queen could have done such a good job. Elizabeth proved that a woman could rule just as well as, and sometimes better than, a man. Future queens would find their lives a lot easier because of her example!

Queen Elizabeth had scarcely taken her last breath when the Scottish king, James, started packing his bags . . .

Meanwhile

• 1562 John Hawkins begins the African slave trade
• 1564 The great playwright William Shakespeare is born
• 1565 The first pencils with black lead are made in England
• 1596 John Harington, the queen's godson, invents the first flushing toilet (the water closet)
• 1599 The Globe Theatre, where Shakespeare's plays were staged, is built in London

James the First

Born 1566 Ruled Scotland 1567 – 1625
England 1603 – 1625

The moment Queen Elizabeth died, the Scottish king, James, rushed down to London to snatch the crown. Elizabeth had no children, and her brother and sisters were all dead, so there was no Tudor heir to the throne. James was a distant cousin from the Stuart family and he wanted to get the crown firmly on his head before anyone else did.

James was a nervous, dishonest, suspicious man with glassy, rolling eyes and a red spotty face. He had some odd ideas – he was frightened of pigs, hated the sea and was forever worrying that witches were casting spells on him! But given his childhood it's not difficult to see why he was so peculiar. In the first year of his life, his father was strangled and then blown up. Shortly afterwards, his mother, Mary Queen of Scots, married the man suspected of being her husband's murderer. James was crowned king of Scotland when he was only thirteen months old. Over the next few years he had various guardians who were shot, poisoned or executed. When he was sixteen he was kidnapped, and when he was twenty his mother's head was cut off by her cousin Elizabeth the First. This was not the best start in life for any boy, let alone a king!

Once he was king of England, James's ambition was to unite England and Scotland. There were still going to be lots of squabbles between the two countries, but once they were sorted out, the new country of Great Britain would be strong enough to take on the world.

Ruled by a pen

When James left Scotland for England he promised he would return regularly to rule Scotland. But he lied. He only went back once in 1617. Instead he received written reports from Scotland and sent back his orders by letter. The people of Scotland joked that they were ruled not by a king but by a pen!

Fireworks!

James was always suspicious that people were plotting against him, and he was right! On the fifth of November, two years after he was crowned, some Catholic terrorists tried to blow up the king and Parliament. But the night before the planned explosion, one of them, Guy Fawkes, was discovered in a cellar under the Houses of Parliament with thirty-six barrels of gunpowder. Guy was tortured, and nearly all the terrorists were captured and executed. The Gunpowder Plot was then used as an excuse to persecute the powerful old Catholic families.

Guy could never have guessed that his capture and grizzly death would still be celebrated 400 years later. Every November, children make a dummy, or Guy, out of old clothes, and burn him on a big bonfire accompanied by displays of fireworks.

A poor inheritance

King James the First was incredibly extravagant and lavished enormous amounts of money on himself and on presents for his favourites. In one year he spent £36,000 just on clothes. Even at his death no expense was spared and he was given one of the most spectacular funerals ever. The result was that his son Charles inherited a very poor kingdom indeed.

Meanwhile

- 1609 *Tea arrives in England*
- 1622 *Read all about it! Britain's first weekly newspaper, the* Weekly News *appears*

Charles the First

Born 1600 Ruled 1625 – 1649

James's son Charles was small, weedy and had a stammer. He was stuffy and religious – rude words were banned from his court – and he had a lousy sense of humour. The sour-faced Charles cheered up a bit when he married the spirited little French queen, Henrietta Maria, who managed to bring a bit of fun to the court. Both king and queen liked to act in pantomimes, and the queen's jester, a dwarf named Jeffrey, would entertain them at feasts – once leaping from a pie wearing a full suit of armour.

Charles was always short of money. He got involved in expensive foreign wars and thought he had the right to spend as much as he wanted. He believed he was chosen by God to be king, and so everyone should do as he said. But the men of Parliament believed Charles was on the side of the Catholics, and they didn't want to give him money for weapons in case he turned his guns on Parliament. Things got worse when Charles tried to get cash from people without asking Parliament's permission. If they refused, he fined them. Then, if they still refused, he put them in prison and cut their ears off!

Finally, the king ordered his soldiers to arrest five of his enemies in Parliament and their supporters. Parliament then called for volunteers to defend it, and a full-scale war broke out.

The King loses his head

Parliament's general, Oliver Cromwell, decided the army wasn't good enough. He weeded out his weakest officers, retrained his men and created a new model army that was loyal, not to Parliament, but to him. This army beat Charles's men and the king fled to his friends the Scots for help. Unfortunately, they weren't very good friends – they sold him back to Cromwell who locked him up in a castle on the Isle of Wight.

Even in prison, Charles plotted and schemed and soon war broke out again. Oliver Cromwell won this time too, but the army decided that there would never be peace as long as the king was alive. King Charles was sentenced to death, and his head was chopped off.

Now there was no king. Would Parliament choose a new one? Would the army run the country? Would one of Charles's relatives invade? Nobody knew. Anything could happen now.

Chilly Charles

When Charles was on his way to the scaffold he asked if he could borrow someone's shirt. He was already wearing one, but it was a cold day and he wanted to get warm so he could stop shivering. He didn't want people to think he was shaking from fear. He still had his head chopped off, but at least he wasn't chilly.

Meanwhile

• 1642 Dutch sailor *Abel Tasman discovers Tasmania – but misses nearby Australia!*

The time of no king at all

1649 – 1660

Young Charles marches on England

As soon as Charles the First's head was chopped off, his son, also called Charles, was declared king by his father's supporters. He joined forces with the Scots and marched on England, but Cromwell's men thrashed them.

As Charles was fleeing he was almost caught by a troop of Cromwell's soldiers. He climbed up a nearby oak tree and hid in the branches. The soldiers stopped under the tree and talked about their plans for catching Charles, then rode off to search nearby farms. He climbed down and ran the other way as fast as he could.

The man who held the country together

All over the country more rows were breaking out. Some people wanted a new king, others never wanted to see another king again. Some people wanted a country in which everyone could do what they wanted. Others wanted to ban anyone whose religion they didn't agree with.

The one man who held the country together was Oliver Cromwell. He was honest and fair, a good general who was respected by everyone. He ran the country well, won lots of foreign wars and was feared by kings all over Europe. Under his rule, English merchants began to make a great deal of money.

Unhappy Ireland

Not everyone thought that Oliver Cromwell was such a great guy. Now that he had a big, new army he decided to send it to Ireland to attack the Catholics who lived there. This was supposedly in retaliation for the Catholic massacre of 3,000 Irish Protestants that had happened eight years earlier. But Cromwell's attack was worse than anything Ireland had ever seen. Every building was destroyed and every field was burned. Thousands were killed without mercy and those left were starved into giving in.

The best king the country never had

Oliver Cromwell was so good at running the country that he was made Lord Protector, which meant he had as much power as most kings. But he would never accept the crown, even though Parliament asked him to be king. Then he died, and the rows broke out more furiously then ever.

King Charles

Cavaliers

Many of the nobles who had supported King Charles the First against Cromwell, wore wide-brimmed hats and had long flowing hair. The Roundheads thought they were just playing at being soldiers so they nicknamed them 'Cavaliers' which means 'not really serious'.

Oliver Cromwell

Roundheads

Oliver Cromwell and a lot of his supporters were Puritans. They believed they had God on their side, hated celebrations like Christmas and birthdays and wore their hair cropped short to show that they weren't vain. The Cavaliers nicknamed them 'Roundheads'.

A punch on the nose

There is a legend that Charles the First and Oliver Cromwell met when they were toddlers and Oliver promptly punched the baby prince in the face and made his nose bleed!

Busy body

When Oliver died he was given a huge state funeral in Westminster Abbey. But later, when England started having kings again, his body was dug up, his head chopped off, and the rest of him hung from a gallows for everyone to see. His head was stuck on a pole outside Westminster Hall, where it stayed for twenty years. Then it blew down in a gale,

and for hundreds of years it passed from one person to another, and was sold, swapped, lost and stolen. Finally, it ended up at the Cambridge college where Oliver had been a student. It now lies buried near the college chapel, but no one will say exactly where, just in case someone steals it again.

The worst king the country never had

Oliver's son Richard was now made Lord Protector, just as though Oliver had been king and had passed the crown to his rightful heir. Even people who didn't believe in kings accepted this, which seems a bit odd. But Richard was a quiet, weak man – a farmer – who wasn't really interested in running the country. No one respected him and within a year he got the sack. Parliament was now split; the army was split. The country was like a ship without a rudder.

Then young Charles the Second, who had been hiding in France, wrote a polite letter home saying what a great fan he was of parliaments. If he was invited back, he said, Parliament would have a big say in how things were run. So Parliament welcomed him back with open arms. All over the country people cheered his return. The Stuart family was back on the throne, but from now on Parliament was going to become more and more powerful.

Charles the Second

Born 1630 Ruled 1660 – 1685

Charles the Second's lifelong ambition had been to get back the throne. But once he got it back, there wasn't a lot he wanted to do with it. He certainly *looked* like a king. He was tall and swarthy with lively, sparkling eyes and a mane of thick black curly hair. He also had the manners of a king, with lots of elaborate gestures. But he wasn't very interested in running a country. He was happier lolling about on cushions, or hunting and horse racing, and going out with other women behind his wife's back.

People thought Charles was a secret Roman Catholic. But he denied this furiously, saying it was 'an absolute, complete, monumental lie'. They were even more suspicious of his brother James, who they suspected was involved in a plot to turn the whole of England Catholic again. Parliament passed a law saying that James could never be king, so Charles closed Parliament down.

Its members were furious. This king seemed as bad as his father! Would they have to fight a civil war all over again? No, Charles did them a favour and had a heart attack. On his deathbed a priest was smuggled into the palace so that Charles could become a Catholic. So much for the absolute, complete, monumental lie!

Seldom has a king had such a promising start and yet died detested by so many people. Unfortunately, an even more un-popular man was about to become king – his brother James.

Bad medicine

One morning in February 1685, Charles woke up feeling very ill and his doctors were called to his bedside. But doctors in those days had some strange ideas! His veins were cut open and he was made to bleed; they put cream made of tar, herbs and pigeon droppings on his feet, and gave him a medicine of crushed human skulls, parts of animals and herbs. By the time they had finished with him he felt a lot worse and, not surprisingly, he died a few days later.

Hair today

Charles's long mane of curly black hair was so admired that his nobles began copying him by wearing wigs. There was such a demand that wig makers started to snatch poor children off the street and shave their heads in order to steal their hair.

'Bring out your dead!'

A dreadful disease called the Great Plague broke out in Charles's reign. Around 100,000 people died in London alone. Carts were driven round the streets each night to collect the dead bodies, their drivers crying, 'Bring out your dead! Bring out your dead!'

London's burning!

The following year, the Great Fire of London raged through the city. Only a few people were killed, but 13,000 houses, eighty-nine churches and four stone bridges were destroyed. London was rebuilt in brick and stone, rather than wood. The streets were made wider and straighter, and straw was no longer used to cover floors. The result was that the city became much cleaner, and the plague never returned.

Meanwhile

• 1687 Isaac Newton discovers the law of gravity — what goes up must come down

James the Second

Born 1633 Ruled 1685 – 1688

Charles the Second had lots of children, but none by the queen. So when he died, his brother James became king. James the Second was a religious man, but he wasn't very holy. He was proud, bossy and big-headed and always had a sneering expression on his face. He had lots of girlfriends, even though he was married. As people had suspected, James had become a Catholic and as soon as he was crowned, he started sacking Protestants from the top jobs and giving them to Catholics instead. Parliament detested the new king. However, it felt fairly smug because James and his wife, Mary of Modena, had no children, so when he died they would just look around for a suitable Protestant to take over.

Then disaster struck. Mary gave birth to a baby boy, although it was rumoured that the baby was really the son of a miller who had been smuggled into the queen's bedroom in a warming pan. Parliament realised that it would have to take drastic action if it wanted to be rid of this Catholic royal family.

Parliament decided to look around for someone else to take charge. It found not one but two people. James had two daughters from a previous marriage and the older one, Mary, was a Protestant who had married William of Orange, the ruler of Holland. Some leading Englishmen wrote to William and Mary and asked them to rule England instead of James. Amazingly, haughty, bossy James backed down as soon as he heard about the letter. He started sacking the Catholics he'd only recently promoted. Then, when William and his army landed in England, James panicked and fled to France, terrified of having his head chopped off.

The feet that got up his nose

There had long been a tradition that the Thursday before Easter, the king of England would wash the feet of some specially chosen poor people to show that he wasn't vain and that he cared for his subjects. But James the Second was too proud to do this and he certainly wasn't going to go near anyone's smelly feet. So he got his servants to do it instead. Nowadays the queen hands out small silver coins on the same Thursday, and she carries a small bunch of flowers in memory of the flowers that the king carried hundreds of years ago to ward off the dreadful cheesy smell.

William the Third and Mary the Second

William born 1650 Ruled 1688 – 1702

Mary born 1662

When Charles's daughter, Mary, was told she had to marry William of Orange, she burst into tears. He was short, with a yellowish face, round shoulders and an annoying cough. She must have thought he was an ugly old troll. When they first met, he didn't like her very much either, and kept a girlfriend throughout their marriage. But as time went by they grew more and more fond of each other.

When William and Mary arrived in Britain from their home in Holland they were greeted with cheers and waving flags. But very soon the usual rows broke out. William wanted money to fight the French; Parliament wanted more say in how the country was run. Then Mary died of smallpox. William was very sad, and kept her wedding ring and a lock of her hair under his clothes for the rest of his life.

Parliament got stronger and William grew more and more miserable. He would happily have given up ruling England and gone back to Holland. Then one day he was out riding when his horse tripped over a mole hill and threw him. William broke his collar bone, got an infection in his lungs and died.

William of Orange

Why was William named after a large, round edible thing that lives in a fruitbowl? Because as well as being ruler of Holland, he was also prince of a small part of France called Orange.

Not for two pins

William was plagued with illness in old age. His body was very thin, but his legs were hugely bloated and painful. His doctor told him that 'I would not have your legs for your three kingdoms.'

Blood Orange

When James the Second escaped to France, he had a great time hunting and dancing and visiting his various girlfriends. After some weeks he had to be reminded that he hadn't yet lost Ireland. He landed there and trained an army. He faced William's troops at the Battle of the Boyne, near Dublin. In blazing heat, William's Protestants won, and the English took full control of Ireland. Today Northern Ireland is still ruled by Britain. Most Catholics think this is wrong, but most Protestants think it is right and some call themselves Orangemen in memory of William's victory.

The Glencoe Massacre

There were many Scots who didn't want William to be king and so they started rebelling. William said he would pardon them if they gave in by 1st January 1672.

The chief of the McDonalds of Glencoe went to the wrong place to make his peace, got delayed by snow and arrived six days late. The Scots who supported William said he hadn't surrendered in time, so the McDonalds must be punished. William's soldiers had been lodging with the McDonalds, but now they were ordered to seal up the valley where the McDonalds lived and kill every last one of them. Many McDonalds died that day, and only a few escaped over the hills in a snowstorm. William himself signed the order for the massacre. Scotland was now firmly under William's control, but the cost had been high in Scottish blood.

Party time

Parliament was full of little gangs who met up to plot how to get their own way. Under William and Mary, two big gangs arose. They became known as 'parties' – although there were no games or birthday cakes. The Whig party wanted a less powerful king and a strong Parliament, the Tory party wanted a strong king and a weaker Parliament. From now on whenever England's rulers needed money they had to find a way of siding with one party without upsetting the other, which wasn't easy to do!

Queen Anne

Born 1665 Ruled 1702 – 1714

When William of Orange died, Mary's sister, Anne, was crowned queen of England, Scotland, Wales and Ireland. This was a grand title for someone as shy and short-sighted as she was, but she turned out to be a big success. Her army won lots of battles, and seized more foreign lands to turn into British colonies. Surprisingly, she was the most popular monarch since Queen Elizabeth the First. But she had a small group of friends who could be extremely horrible to her. Even her best friend, the Duchess of Marlborough, once told her to shut up, which wasn't something you were supposed to say to a queen!

As she got older Anne became very ill. Her foot swelled up, her face turned red and spotty and she grew so fat she had to be hoisted onto her throne. In public she got all the glory, but in private she was deeply miserable and became addicted to brandy. She and her husband, Prince George, had several children but the eldest only lived to the age of eleven, and Anne was heartbroken when her husband died a few years later. When Anne died the Stuart royal family came to an end.

Not so magic queen

For hundreds of years people thought kings and queens were magical. In England it was believed that the royal touch could make people better. The king would stroke a sick person's cheeks and throat with both hands, and this was supposed to cure them. Anne was the last monarch to do this. She stroked lots of people who had a particularly disgusting disease called scrofula. But this didn't seem to do them any good at all. So the custom died out. More and more people were beginning to think of the royal family, not as God-like creatures, but as human beings like themselves.

George the First

Born 1660 Ruled 1714 – 1727

There were over fifty people, all relatives of the Stuarts, who had a better claim to the throne than George, Duke of Hanover. So how did such a boring, elderly German who spoke almost no English become king? The answer is that he was the grandson of James the First, and a Protestant, and all the other people who had a better claim to the throne were Catholics. They couldn't be king because Parliament had passed a law saying that no Catholic could rule England.

Things were calmer in England during George's reign. There were wars with other countries, of course, and English merchants were making so much money abroad that fortunes were made very quickly and then lost even faster. But there weren't the furious rows with Parliament that there had been under the Stuarts. This was mainly because George was much more interested in his German home than he was in England and went back there as often as he could. He had a son, also called George, with whom he was always squabbling, but who he still wanted to succeed him. And when George the First died, few people wanted to go back to the hectic Stuart days. So George the Second became king without a fight.

Not king, just pretending (part one)

James the Second had a son who never became king because he was a Catholic. His name was James Frances Edward and he was known as 'the Old Pretender' because he pretended to be king when someone else sat on the throne. A lot of people, particularly Catholics, would have liked him to be their ruler. They were called Jacobites and were ready to rise up and fight for him. The trouble was that James was a bit of a baby. The first time he set off for England he got measles and went home again. The second time he caught a sniffly cold and didn't feel well enough to fight. Finally, when George the First died and James had a really good chance of being made king, he went into hiding for three weeks. The Jacobites lost faith in The Old Pretender after that, and had to wait thirty years for a new hero – the Young Pretender!

The first Prime Minister

George spent so much time in Germany that he left the running of the country to his first minister, Robert Walpole – who was, therefore, Britain's first prime minister.

Death by strawberry

George the First died of a heart attack caused by terrible diarrhoea brought on by eating too many strawberries.

Meanwhile

• 1719 Daniel Defoe publishes Robinson Crusoe

George the Second

Born 1683 Ruled 1727 – 1760

When George the Second was Prince of Wales he told everyone at court how much he loved England, and what a tiresome place his homeland Hanover was. But as soon as he was crowned he changed his tune. Suddenly, German cooking was really tasty, and English cooking made you throw up; German horses were ten times faster than English ones and German girls were more polite, more sensible and two hundred times prettier than English girls. Understandably, this sort of attitude didn't go down too well!

George the Second was also rude and rather fierce, and although he was short, he was quite vain and even boasted that he had gorgeous legs! But he could be sensible, if a bit lazy, and was the last British king to lead an army into battle. For much of his life he let Parliament rule the country while he played cards, went hunting, or holidayed in Hanover. Towards the end of George's reign, his army began fighting with France in order to get control of land overseas. Britain had some very good generals and won Canada and vast territories in India. By the time the war was over, Britain had more colonies than any other nation. In fact, it was no longer just a collection of colonies; Britain was now a fabulously wealthy empire!

Not king, just pretending (part two)

Three years after his father James 'the Old Pretender' had tried to seize the crown, Charles Edward Stuart – nicknamed 'Bonnie Prince Charlie' – landed in Scotland with a small army. The Scots rallied round him. He captured the Scottish capital of Edinburgh and forged south for England. He tried to get the English on his side, but hardly anyone wanted to join him. His generals told him that if he didn't retreat his army would be slaughtered. And they were right. Charles Stuart replied that if he retreated he would never be king, and he was right too. His army headed back to Scotland and was horribly massacred at the Battle of Culloden by the king's son, the Duke of Cumberland.

Bonnie Prince Charlie escaped to France. He never returned to Britain and there were no more Jacobite rebellions. At last the Scots and the English had no reason to fight each other. Great Britain could now concentrate on becoming the most powerful nation in the world.

Big wig

Georgian ladies went in for big hair! They would build up their own hair with wigs and then make it even bigger using cushions, paste, animal fat and feathers. Perhaps it's not surprising that insects and even mice could be found nesting in these smelly constructions!

Death by chocolate

One morning King George was sitting on the lavatory drinking a cup of hot chocolate when he had a massive heart attack and dropped dead on the spot.

Meanwhile

- *1744 First record of a cricket match*
- *1754 The Earl of Sandwich invents . . . the sandwich!*

George the Third

Born 1738   Ruled 1760 — 1820

UNLIKE HIS FATHER AND HIS GRANDFATHER, GEORGE number three didn't rush off to Hanover all the time. He had grown up in England and considered himself an Englishman through and through. He was religious, adored being with his family and took the job of being king very seriously. He loved England so much he hardly ever went anywhere else – his idea of a wonderful holiday was a fortnight in Weymouth with his huge family. But even though he didn't travel very far people felt as if they knew him. For the first time there were lots of newspapers and they all carried stories about him. People knew what he looked like too, because there was more money than ever before and his face was on every coin. The whole country knew the new national anthem 'God Save the King'.

Towards the end of his life George got a disease of the blood and went mad. Sometimes this was very funny – he once had a chat with a tree which he thought was the King of Prussia. But sometimes he was scary and his wife, Charlotte, became so frightened of him that she couldn't bear to be near him. At last his son, another George, (surprise, surprise!) became regent and ran the country for him.

George the Third's last years were very sad. He would wander the corridors of Windsor Castle wearing an old dressing gown. Then he would bash out a tune on his battered old harpsichord and tell everyone it was the favourite song of a mad old king who was now dead.

Family parade

George the Third and his queen, Charlotte, produced more princes and princesses than any other British royal family – fifteen in all. When staying at Windsor Castle, the king would make them all parade up and down on the terrace in order of height, the babies being carried by their nursemaids.

What's brewing? A harbour full of tea

The colonies in America grew even larger and richer under George the Third. But there was one problem. The British had to spend vast sums of money on soldiers to protect the

colonists. Parliament had a plan. In order that the colonists should pay some of the bills, it invented lots of taxes. But the colonists had no intention of paying. There was big trouble brewing. A British boat sailed into Boston harbour full of tea, on which the Americans were supposed to pay tax. Some colonists dressed up as American Indians, climbed on board under cover of night and 342 chests of British tea ended up floating in the harbour.

This led to a full-scale war between Britain and the Americans. But the colonists soon realised that they didn't just want to be free of taxes, they wanted to be free of Britain too. No one was sure who would win, but when the Spanish and French joined in on the colonists' side, George was forced to sign a peace treaty and give the Americans their freedom. Parliament's plan had completely failed. The king had always thought he was surrounded by useless politicians. Now he knew he was!

The Union Jack

In 1801 the Irish Parliament was united with the British one. Ever since, the British flag has been made up of three crosses: St George's for England, St Andrew's for Scotland and St Patrick's for Ireland.

Why don't the British speak French?

During George the Third's reign a huge war broke out with France. The French had revolted against their king and cut his head off. They now had a new leader, Napoleon Bonaparte, who had a massive army and a passionate wish to conquer the whole of Europe – including Britain. The country was in real danger and needed good leaders. What did it have instead? A mad king, a weak Prince Regent who took drugs and drank too much, and a Parliament that never stopped arguing. But it did have two brilliant commanders, Lord Nelson, who won the Battle of Trafalgar, and the Duke of Wellington who won the battle of Waterloo. Without them the French would probably have totally defeated Britain and the British would now say 'Bonjour' instead of 'Hello'.

Goodbye Farmer George

George the Third's last days were spent quietly in a darkened room at Windsor Castle, although he still sometimes had outbursts of mania – when his servants tried to shave him he threatened to bring in the battle-axes! He loved the countryside and the simple things of life, and died peacefully, a sad old man of whom people had grown rather fond and who they called 'Farmer George'.

Meanwhile

- *1770 James Cook discovers Australia*
- *1765 First known children's picture book, Goody Two Shoes is published*
- *1785 Edmund Cartwright invents the power loom*
- *1789 French Revolution begins*
- *1789 George Washington becomes the first president of America*

George the Fourth

Born 1762 Regent 1811 – 1820
Ruled 1820 – 1830

George's son, George the Fourth, was spoilt, selfish and vain. When he was young he was always in trouble. He got into terrible debt, then fell in love with a widow called Maria Fitzherbert and married her. His father was furious because she was Catholic. Parliament promised to pay George's debts if he divorced her, so he did and married his cousin, Princess Caroline of Brunswick. But they couldn't stand each other, so she packed her bags and left for Europe.

While he was regent, George spent a fortune on paintings and swanky new buildings, including a great domed pavilion in Brighton that looked like Aladdin's palace. Britain was in the middle of a big war and people were suffering, but George spent more and more money on himself and became very unpopular.

By the time he became king, George was not a very majestic figure. He wore horrible greasy make-up on his face and was so fat it was said that his stomach hung down to his knees. It didn't help that he began to stay in bed all day where he was served huge meals. Because he was such a weak king he couldn't do anything to stop the big changes that were starting to happen. A law was passed allowing Catholics to vote in elections, and another law allowed ordinary people to go on strike to try to get better wages and conditions from cruel and greedy bosses. Up till now, only a few people had had a say in running the country. Soon millions would. Maybe a stronger king could have stopped this happening, but George the Fourth certainly couldn't. Sometimes weak kings can be rather useful.

Smelly knickers

Probably one of the reasons George the Fourth didn't fall madly in love with his new bride, Princess Caroline, was that she hardly ever washed her underwear and smelled horrible!

Tall story

In later life George had a woman friend, Lady Conningham, who was as fat and silly as the king himself. They both doted on a giraffe that had been a present from Egypt, and cartoons appeared in the newspapers about their stupid behavior.

Princess nuisance

When George became king, his wife, Princess Caroline, decided to come back to England to make trouble for him. This was a problem for two reasons. Firstly because he detested her; secondly because for the past few years she had been a party girl and had a boyfriend. Parliament promised her £50,000 a year if she stayed away, but she refused. Her presence was very embarrassing. But the public loved her and cheered her wherever she went. She even tried to get into Westminster Abbey when her husband was being crowned, but was told to go away. She died a month later of a stomach problem.

Meanwhile

- 1812 The Grimm brothers publish their first book of fairy tales
- 1816 Jane Austen publishes Emma — and is forced to dedicate it to the king at his request (even though she couldn't stand him!)
- 1820 Florence Nightingale is born
- 1825 George Stephenson builds the first public steam railway
- 1827 Strike a light — matches are invented
- 1829 Robert Peel founds the first police force in London

William the Fourth

Born 1765 Ruled 1830 — 1837

George the Fourth had a daughter, Charlotte, who was his heir, and two brothers, Frederick and William. Nobody expected William to become king, so he didn't get any proper training. He was sent away to sea when he was thirteen, and was made Admiral of the Fleet just before he retired to become king. He was poor, had few friends and had an annoying habit of wiping his nose with his finger.

Before he became king, he lived with an actress. He never married her, but they had ten children to support and he was always penniless. Then both Charlotte and Frederick died, and William suddenly became heir to the throne. He dumped his actress and married the wealthy Princess Adelaide so he could pay off his debts and supply the country with some princes and princesses.

Then when the ghastly George the Fourth died, William was crowned king. Perhaps it's not surprising that he didn't know how to behave at George's funeral. He talked loudly and nonstop to anyone who would listen, and spent the following days driving around in an open carriage bowing to the crowds. People called him 'the Sailor King' because of his time in the Navy. But his family called him 'Silly Billy'.

A less powerful king

Many people were unhappy that the king still had quite a lot of power. They wanted to choose members of Parliament themselves so they could have a say in how the country was run. King William, of course, wanted to keep

things as they were but Parliament decided that more people should be allowed to vote and the king couldn't stop it happening. If someone had suggested to Henry the Eighth or Elizabeth the First that ordinary people should have a vote, they'd have had their heads chopped off. But times had changed and there was no going back.

The Common King

Because William had no royal training his behaviour seemed strange and alarming to his courtiers. He would spit in public and wore great big Wellington boots because he believed they guarded him against chills. He would often stop his carriage to ask complete strangers if they wanted a lift and allowed himself to be hugged and kissed by women in the street.

The end of the line

William eventually learned a few things about being a king, but not much. He certainly wasn't one of Britain's great kings and many people thought he was a bit of a joke. William and Adelaide had two daughters but they died before the king. So the next monarch was his niece Victoria – and what a queen she turned out to be!

Meanwhile

- 1834 *Cyrus McCormick invents the first harvesting machine*
- 1834 *Slavery is abolished in the British Empire*
- 1836 *Charles Dickens publishes* The Pickwick Papers
- 1836 *The city of Adelaide, named after William the Fourth's wife, is founded in Australia*

Queen Victoria

Born 1819   Ruled 1837 – 1901

FIVE GRUMPY OLD MEN HAD SAT ON THE THRONE before Victoria, so the new young queen was a breath of fresh air. She was eighteen, tiny, serious and really wanted to be good at her job. So no one minded when she fell madly in love and married a German prince, Albert, who couldn't even speak English properly. But that was only half the story. Victoria had a terrible temper and could be as obstinate as a mule. Throughout her reign there were blazing rows with everyone from her nine children to the Prime Minister.

Victoria wanted Albert to be her king, but Parliament wouldn't let him, so he was given the special title of 'Prince Consort' instead, which didn't mean much at all. He was a very serious man who believed in duty, and his duty was to work hard for his new subjects. Perhaps he worked too hard. One cold winter he caught typhoid and died at the age of forty-two. Victoria was heartbroken. She dressed all in black and wouldn't leave the palace. Years went by. The public grew restless. They wanted a proper queen, not one who hid away all the time. People began to wonder if they needed a royal family at all.

Eventually, she was coaxed out of the palace and the crowds began to cheer her again. At her Diamond Jubilee, Victoria celebrated sixty years of glorious rule and most people couldn't remember a time when she hadn't been there. She was terribly patriotic and to her mind Britain was always right and she said so, very firmly, even when it was wrong! Britain had conquered so much land abroad that the queen now ruled over 400 million people from the great sub-continent of India, where she was empress, to Canada, Australia and New Zealand. The British Empire was now so huge it made up over a fifth of the whole world. By the time she died, little old Queen Victoria had become as famous as that other great queen, Elizabeth the First.

A new royal family

When Victoria's uncle William the Fourth died it marked the end of the Hanovers. Victoria's German mother was a Saxe-Coburg and so was her adored husband Alfred. So the Saxe-Coburgs were now the new royal family.

A fortune told

Before Victoria was even born, a gypsy told her father that he would have a daughter who would become a great queen.

Bloomin' bloomers

Victoria was not a fan of women's rights. It made her furious even to think of women having such ideas. When Amelia Bloomer tried to make baggy pants (bloomers) popular the queen was almost speechless with rage at the thought of women in trousers!

The queen's favourite

Victoria had a favourite servant, a Scot called John Brown. The public were very suspicious of him because he seemed to have tremendous power over the queen. They thought he might be her secret boyfriend. He wore a kilt everywhere and was drunk a lot of the time. But the queen adored him and ordered a lock of his hair to be buried with her in a secret compartment of her coffin.

John saves the queen

Queen Victoria was in an open carriage with two of her young sons when a man dashed out of the crowd and pointed a gun at her! Immediately, John Brown grabbed him and wrestled him to the ground. It was discovered later that the gun hadn't been loaded – but the queen always insisted that John had saved her life.

A naughty little boy

Victoria was very fond of her grandson William. 'Such a dear, good little boy,' she wrote. But during the wedding of her eldest son, he managed to dig the jewel out of his dagger and throw it at his uncles to annoy them, and when they caught him he bit their legs. When he grew up, he annoyed them even more. He became Kaiser Wilhelm the Second who led Germany against England in the First World War!

The Great Exhibition

The 1850s were a time of exciting new inventions. Albert loved this new technology and decided to mount an enormous exhibition to show it off. It was held in London's Hyde Park, in a vast, specially built glass building called the Crystal Palace. The following year the whole building was taken down and rebuilt on a new site on the outskirts of London. Soon the whole area surrounding it became known as Crystal Palace and that is what it's still called today.

Goodbye dear Albert

When Prince Albert died, Victoria was determined to make the biggest and best statue of him that she could. The Albert Memorial took eight years to build and was made with marble, real gold leaf and semi-precious stones. You can still see it today in Hyde Park in London.

'The queen speaking . . .'

Victoria liked to keep up with all the latest inventions. She had the first shower installed in Sandringham and made Alexander Bell visit her at Osborne to demonstrate his amazing new machine – the telephone.

A new century

When Victoria was born, stagecoaches had rattled through Britain. By the time she died the country was criss-crossed by a network of new roads and railways, and wonderful new inventions were happening all the time. The royal family seemed to be the one thing that never changed (even though it was actually changing all the time).

Victoria died aged eighty-one surrounded by dozens of children, grandchildren and great-grandchildren. It was 1901 and a new century had begun. Everyone knew that with the queen, an era had passed. Her roly-poly son, Albert Edward, was about to become king, and change his name.

Meanwhile

• 1839 *Louis Daguerre invents photography*
• 1851 *Isaac Singer invents the sewing machine*
• 1855 *Dr Livingstone discovers Victoria Falls*
• 1859 *Charles Darwin publishes his theory of evolution — everyone is outraged at the idea that humans are descended from apes!*
• 1865 *Pierre Lalement invents the bicycle (bone-shaker)*
• 1870 *Spain and Prussia at war*
• 1877 *Thomas Edison invents the record player*
• 1878 *Thomas Edison invents the electric light*
• 1885 *Karl Benz invents the motor car*
• 1888 *First moving picture is shown*
• 1895 *Marconi invents the radio*
• 1898 *Marie Curie discovers radiation*
• 1900 *A new political party is founded to represent working people - the Labour Party*

Edward the Seventh

Born 1841 Ruled 1901 – 1910

Edward was an old man of almost sixty when he came to the throne. He had thought his mother, Queen Victoria, was old-fashioned and stubborn. She had thought he was lazy and silly. They were probably both right. Edward had been christened Albert Edward, but he didn't want the same name as his mother's beloved husband, so when she died he dropped his first name.

As a little boy, he was such a bully that his brothers and sisters were scared of him. He made faces, spat and threw stones at his teacher. When he grew up he got fat, grew a beard and looked like a jolly old gentleman. But he wasn't. His idea of a good joke was to pour his brandy over someone's head, or stub his cigar out on their hand. His favourite place in the world was his country estate at Sandringham in Norfolk. He liked shooting animals there. In one day his hunting party shot 3,000 birds, on another day 6,000 rabbits. A few animals were luckier. He adored his little fox terrier Caesar so much he took him everywhere and even had his collar inscribed with the motto 'I belong to the king.'

You might think that Edward's subjects would have found him rather revolting, but they didn't. They called him 'Good old Teddy' and loved reading about his gambling, his expensive parties, and the rich young lords and ladies who were his friends. He married a beautiful Danish princess, Alexandra, although he continued to have lots of girlfriends.

Edward died after a heart attack brought on by bronchitis, which isn't surprising. He ate a lot, drank a lot, smoked twelve huge cigars a day, plus cigarettes. Soon, not only was he dead, but the whole glamorous world in which he lived passed away too. The First World War destroyed it all.

Meanwhile

• 1901 *The Earl of Hopetown becomes the first Governor General of Australia*

• 1903 *The Wright brothers invent the aeroplane*

• 1903 *Emmeline Pankhurst founds the Suffragette Movement to campaign for votes for women. One of its members, Emily Davison, throws herself under the king's horse at the Derby and is killed.*

George the Fifth

Born 1865 Ruled 1910 – 1936

George the Fifth was Edward's second son. Like his grandmother, Queen Victoria, George liked simple things. His hobby was stamp collecting and he would rather stay at home in his slippers than go out to fancy parties. He was also keen to be a good king. In other words, he was a decent chap (although unlike Queen Victoria he swore a lot).

While he was king the First World War broke out. For four years the British fought the Germans and millions of soldiers died. So much money was spent on this war and so many young lives were lost that Britain would never be the same again. Lots of people hated the Germans for this. George was worried that they might start hating the royal family too because they were called the Saxe-Coburgs, which was a German name. So he changed his name to George Windsor, which was the name of a castle near London. The royal family are still known as the Windsors to this day.

Not quite independent Ireland

The English had ruled Ireland since the days of Elizabeth the First. Many Irish people resented this and were angry that Catholics were banned from taking part in government. By the time of George the Fifth, most people wanted Ireland to separate from Britain and form a new country. Britain gave southern Ireland its independence, but six counties in the north stayed as part of Britain. This was to cause more trouble than anyone could have imagined at the time.

Meanwhile

• 1914-18 *First World War*
• 1917 *Mohandas Gandhi begins campaign seeking India's independence from Britain*
• 1922 *Egypt wins independence from Britain*
• 1926 *John Logie Baird invents television*

• 1928 *All women over twenty-one are given the vote*
• 1928 *Mickey Mouse appears in his first cartoon*
• 1928 *Alexander Fleming discovers penicillin*
• 1930 *First World Cup held in and won by Uruguay*

Edward the Eighth

Born 1894 Ruled January 1936 — December 1936

George the Fifth's son Edward liked golf, wine, big dinners and nightclubs, and often looked bored to death when he was performing his kingly duties. But he was charming and good-looking, with fair hair and sad blue eyes, so people liked him.

He fell madly in love with a woman called Wallis Simpson and could see no reason why she shouldn't be his queen. Unfortunately, Parliament didn't feel the same. Mrs Simpson wasn't a princess, she wasn't even from a rich, old European family. She was American and had been divorced not once, but twice. Parliament didn't think she was the right sort of person to be queen. The Prime Minister told Edward he could have the throne or Mrs Simpson, but not both. Edward was so besotted that he chose Mrs Simpson and made a famous broadcast on radio giving up the throne. The crown was taken away from him and he became simply the Duke of Windsor and the couple left England for good and lived abroad for the rest of their lives.

George the Sixth

Born 1895 Ruled 1936 — 1952

The new king had a tough challenge. He had to pick up the pieces after the mess his brother Edward had left behind. At first George didn't like the idea of being king at all, telling an advisor, 'This is terrible, I've had no training!' Even his coronation didn't bode well. When the moment came for him to read out his kingly oath, his bishops couldn't find the right page in the book. When they finally did, the archbishop accidentally put his thumb over the words. Then, as the king got out of his coronation chair, another bishop stood on his robe and poor George nearly fell over.

But as it turned out, there couldn't have been a better man for the job than George the Sixth. You wouldn't have thought so though. He was shy, not especially clever and had a stammer, but both he and his pretty young wife, Elizabeth, became very popular, especially during the Second World War.

Bombs were falling all over London and thousands of people died. London was a very scary place to be, but George and Elizabeth stayed put in Buckingham Palace and wouldn't move, even though two bombs landed on the palace itself. They also visited other towns and cities that had been damaged by the bombing, and met more ordinary people than any king or queen before them. But once the fighting had stopped, was there any kind of useful job left for the king of England? One answer came with the creation of the Commonwealth.

After the war, many of Britain's colonies demanded their freedom and started to rule themselves. But they still wanted to help each other, and they thought they could be quite powerful as a big group. So they set up

their own club called the Commonwealth and King George was formally recognised as its head. From that moment his main job was travelling around the world trying to make the Commonwealth stronger and more united. By the time he died he had helped to do just that. Now nearly everyone thought that keeping the monarchy was a good idea.

The next queen was the eldest of his two young daughters, Elizabeth.

The king who wouldn't go away

After Edward the Eighth left Britain he became a big nuisance. He went to Germany and met its horrible leader Adolf Hitler without asking permission from the British Government. When Britain declared war on Germany, King George ordered Edward to come home. But he wouldn't unless he could bring Mrs Simpson with him. Parliament sent him to the West Indies and made him Governor of the Bahamas. Hitler planned to invade England and put Edward back on the throne. Many people believe Edward would have gone along with this, even though it would have made him a traitor.

Meanwhile

- 1939-1945 *The Second World War*
- 1945 *The first (and hopefully last) atomic bombs are dropped on Japan*
- 1948 *New Jewish state of Israel is proclaimed*
- 1947 *India wins independence from Britain*
- 1949 *Communists seize power in China*

Elizabeth the Second

Born 1926   Ruled 1952 -

AS A CHILD, QUEEN ELIZABETH SEEMED THE PERFECT little princess. She was angelic, rosy-cheeked, and had a mop of curly hair. She really was incredibly well behaved too – it seems one of the naughtiest things she ever did was throw her teddy bear down the stairs! Crowds flocked to see her whenever she appeared in public and people were interested in everything she did – lists of her birthday presents were even printed in the newspapers.

She was ten when her father, George, became king, and as she was next in line to the throne, she had to begin training to be queen. Every bit of her life was planned. She had to attend luncheons and banquets, sit through boring speeches and be polite to everyone she met. She also had to learn foreign languages and lots of history. But her advisors didn't want her to become too grand, so she was taught how to cook, clean and polish as well.

In some ways Elizabeth is a modern Queen Victoria. Like Victoria, she was crowned when she was very young, she's small and serious and works hard. She loves horses and riding, and is devoted to her country and her family. She married a Greek prince called Philip and they have four children, Charles, the heir to the throne, Anne, Andrew and Edward.

For nearly fifty years, Queen Elizabeth has behaved as well as she was taught to as a little girl. She has made countless royal visits and is constantly visiting foreign countries as head of the Commonwealth. And she still has to listen to boring speeches and be polite to everyone. Perhaps being queen is not always the best job in the world.

Record-breaking queen

Queen Elizabeth the Second is one of Britain's longest-reigning monarchs. She has been on the throne longer than any other monarch except Henry the Third (62 years), George the Third and Queen Victoria (60 years).

Kings and queens move into show business

Queen Victoria was the first English queen to be photographed. Edward the Seventh's subjects could see him on silent film and George the Fifth made the first broadcast on radio. Queen Elizabeth's was the first coronation on television and now there is even a Buckingham Palace website!

'Good morning, your majesty!'

In 1982, to everyone's astonishment, a man called Michael Fagan managed to break into Buckingham Palace early one morning and stroll straight into the queen's bedroom. He pulled the curtains, woke up the Queen, then sat on her bed and began telling her about his family! She kept him talking until a footman came and rescued her. Now the palace is guarded much more carefully!

Horses and hounds

Elizabeth's favourite dogs are corgis, even though some of them have bitten her! She also own lots of horses and loves riding and watching horse-racing.

Two queens

In 1979 Britain's first woman Prime Minister, Margaret Thatcher, came to power. Elizabeth was always very polite to her, but most people think she didn't like her very much. Mrs Thatcher was rather grand – perhaps Elizabeth thought she was trying to behave like a queen!

Changing times

Big changes began to happen when the royal advisors made an important decision – one that would affect the royal family forever. The advisors began to think the queen seemed too serious and old-fashioned. So newspaper and television reporters were invited to take lots of pictures of her whole family. At first this worked well, the royal children always seemed to be smiling and happy. And when Prince Charles married Lady Diana Spencer at a dazzling wedding, it seemed like a fairy tale. Then things started to go wrong. First, Princess Anne got divorced and so did her brother Andrew. Then, horror of horrors, Charles and his fairy-tale princess were divorced too. And if that wasn't enough, the beloved Princess Diana was killed in a car crash with her new boyfriend. In the past, the press had only reported happy stories. Now they reported unhappy ones as well. Phones were tapped, servants were bribed to tell tales and photographers got secret pictures of the queen's family misbehaving. Now it seemed that the royal family had the same troubles as the rest of us. Some people thought that if British royalty was going to survive and become popular again, it would have to find a different, more modern way of doing things. Other people wondered if kings and queens had had their day. Perhaps Queen Elizabeth would be the very last queen of England.

Meanwhile

- 1954 Roger Bannister is the first man to run the four minute mile
- 1955 The first British television programmes with advertising begin
- 1959 The first crossing of the English Channel by Hovercraft
- 1964 Roald Dahl publishes his first children's book James and the Giant Peach
- 1966 England's football team win the World Cup

- 1969 Robin Knox-Johnson sails round the world in the first non-stop solo voyage
- 1969 First men land on the moon
- 1974 Britain joins the Common Market
- 1978 Louise Brown, the first test tube baby, is born
- 1982 Britain and Argentina are at war over the Falkland Islands
- 1989 The Berlin Wall is knocked down
- 1991 Britain and UN allies fight Iraq in the Gulf War
- 1994 The Channel Tunnel is opened
- 1994 Apartheid (racial segregation) ends in South Africa and Nelson Mandela becomes President
- 1999 NATO intervenes in Kosovo crisis
- 1999 Prince Edward marries Sophie Rhys-Jones

So what will happen next?

Will Prince Charles become king, but sell his big palaces and live in a little house? Will a distant relative decide he wants to be king instead and seize the throne in a bloody battle? Will people decide they don't want a royal family any more and have a president instead? Or will the royal family do what it has so often done in the past, changing just fast enough to make people think it is special and worth hanging on to. Only time will tell.

Bibliography

D P Kirby, *The Earliest English Kings*, Unwin Hyman; M K Lawson, *Cnut*, Longman; Ian Walher, *Harold: the Last Anglo-Saxon King*, Frome; Else Roesdahl (ed.) *The Vikings in England*, London, The Anglo-Danish Viking Project; Christopher Brooke, *The Saxon and Norman Kings*, Batsford; David Dumville, *Wessex and England from Alfred to Edgar*, Boydell Press; Christine Fell, *Edward, King and Martyr*, University of Leeds; Eleanor Ducheff, *Alfred the Great and his England*, Collins; Douglas Woodruff, *Alfred the Great*, Weidenfeld & Nicolson; Frank Barlow, *Edward the Confessor*, Eyre Methuen; Dorothy Whitelock, *The Norman Conquest*, Eyre & Spottiswode; M T Clancy, *England and its Rulers 1066-1272*, Fontana; John Chambers, *The Norman Kings*, Weidenfeld & Nicolson; Trevor Rowley, *The High Middle Ages 1200 -1550*, Routledge; Robin Frame, *The Political Development of the British Isles 1100-1400*, Clarendon Press; Frank Barlow, *The Feudal Kingdom of England 1042-1216*, Longman; Regine Pernaud, *Eleanor of Aquitaine*, Collins; W L Warren, *King John*, Eyre Methuen; Kate Norgale, *John Lackland*, Macmillan; Janet Nelson, *Richard Coeur de Lion in History and Myth*, King's College; John Gillinghouse. *Richard the Lionheart*, Book Club Associates; Richard Mortimer, *Angevin England 1154-1258*, Basil Blackwell; Tim Bradbury, *Stephen and Matilda: the Civil War of 1139-53*, Sutton; Frank Barlow, *William Rufus*, Methuen; David C Douglas, *William the Conqueror*, Eyre & Spottiswode; Michael Hicks, *Richard III*, Collins; G L Harris, *Henry V*, Eyre and Spottiswode; Rowena Archer (ed.) *Rulers and Ruled in Late Medieval England*, Hambledon Press; James Gillespie, *The Age of Richard II*, Sutton; Christine Carpenter, *The Wars of the Roses*, CUP; Michael Prestwich, *The Three Edwards*, Weidenfeld & Nicolson; Alan Harding, *England in the Thirteenth Century*, CUP, Chris Cook, *Modern British History 1714 - 1987*, Longman; Henri and Barbara van der Zee, *William and Mary*, Macmillan; Lionel K J Glassey (ed.), *The Reigns of Charles II and James VI and II*, Macmillan; D R Watson, *Charles I*, Weidenfeld & Nicolson; Alan G R Smith (ed.), *The Reign of James VI and I*, Macmillan; Robert Ashton, *The English Civil War*, Weidenfeld & Nicolson; K H D Haley, *The Stuarts*, St Martins Press NY; Neville Williams, *Elizabeth I*, Weidenfeld & Nicolson; Christopher Haigh, *Elizabeth I*, Longman; Robert Lacy, *Henry VIII*, Weidenfeld & Nicolson; Roger Lodyer, *Tudor and Stuart Britain 1471-1714*, Longman; Donald Reed, *Edwardian England*, Harrap; David Thomson, *England in the 20th Century*, Pelican; Dorothy Thompson, *Queen Victoria: Gender and Power*, Virago; Philip Ziegler, *King William IV*, Collins, Dorothy Marshall, *Victoria*, Weidenfeld & Nicolson; John Clarke, *George III*, Weidenfeld & Nicolson; Frank O'Gorman, *The Long Eighteenth Century*, Hodder & Stoughton; J H Plumb, *The First Four Georges*, Batsford; Antonia Fraser, *The Six Wives of Henry VIII*; Winston Churchill, *A History of the English Speaking Peoples*; Encyclopaedia Britannica; *Dr Brewer's Guide to English History*, Jarrold & Sons; Cannon and Griffiths, *The British Monarchy*, OUP; *The Medieval Messenger*, Usborne; I R Worsnop, *Stuarts and Georgians*, Basil Blackwell; Roy Strong, *The Story of Britain: A People's History*, Hutchinson; John Cannon and Ralph Griffiths: *The Oxford Illustrated History of the British Monarchy*, OUP; Antonia Fraser (ed.) *The Lives of the Kings & Queens of England*, Weidenfeld & Nicolson; John D Clare (ed.) *Knights in Armour*, Harcourt Brace; John D Clare, *I Was There: Vikings*, Bodley Head; Kenneth O Morgan, *The Oxford Illustrated History of Britain*, OUP; Ian Dawson, *The Tudor Century*, Nelson; Elizabeth Hallam (ed.), *The Plantagenet Chronicles*, Weidenfeld & Nicolson; Ben Pimlott, *The Queen: A Biography of Elizabeth II*, Harper Collins; Vivian Green, *The Madness of Kings*, Sutton; Alison Weir, *The Six Wives of Henry VIII*, Pimlico; Christopher Hibbert, *The Court at Windsor*, Penguin; Alan and Veronica Palmer, *The Chronology of British History*, Century; The Queensberry Group, *The Book of Key Facts*, Paddington; Edith Sitwell, *Victoria of England*, Cresset.

For Laura – my researcher, advisor, critic and friend.
Oh yes, and she's also my daughter so we sometimes get
on each other's nerves a bit – T.R.

First published in 1999

1 3 5 7 9 10 8 6 4 2

Text © Tony Robinson 1999
Illustrations © individual illustrators 1999; see Contents

The author and illustrators have asserted their right under the
Copyright, Designs and Patents Act, 1988

First published in the United Kingdom in 1999 by
Hutchinson Children's Books
The Random House Group Limited
20 Vauxhall Bridge Road
London SW1V 2SA

Random House Australia (Pty) Limited
20 Alfred Street, Milsons Point, Sydney
New South Wales 2061, Australia

Random House New Zealand Limited
18 Poland Road, Glenfield
Auckland 10, New Zealand

Random House South Africa (Pty) Limited
Endulini, 5A Jubilee Road, Parktown 2193, South Africa

The Random House Group Limited Reg. No. 954009

A CIP catalogue record for this book is available from the British Library

ISBN: 0 09 176804 7

Printed and bound in Italy by Lego SpA